From Inmate to Advocate:
A Journey of Transformation

A Journey of Transformation takes you through 12 pivotal chapters, each paired with a heartfelt poem. These chapters reveal hard truths. Through his own life and penmanship, the author, Edward A. Julian, Sr personally shares challenging tests and trials, including how he overcame his 14 years in federal prison. From moments of doubt to breakthroughs of hope, this book is not just about his journey, but the possibilities that await anyone willing to embrace change. Edward's words remind us

"Transformation isn't a single event; instead it's an ongoing, often grueling journey of facing yourself, confronting your past, and owning your choices." His call for change is for both the incarcerated and those responsible for the policies and practices that keep them jailed. This book has inspired people from all walks of life, including those in positions of authority and power.

edwardajuliansr.com

Praise for Edward A. Julian, Sr

<><><><><><><><><><><><><>

Since 2017, Think Make Live Youth has been dedicated to building opportunities that empower young people. Over the past year, Edward A. Julian, Sr has become an invaluable part of our team as a credible messenger. His commitment, resilience, and genuine connection with youth set him apart.

Whether working in our school-based initiatives or leading the Think Make Live Youth Guns Down summer program, Edward has consistently motivated students to shift their mindset, make constructive decisions, and live intentionally. His powerful journey of personal growth, paired with a deep passion for mentorship, continues to leave a profound impact on the lives of the young individuals we serve. I'm honored to work alongside him and look forward to the lasting difference his leadership will bring.

— Terry Green Founder & CEO,
Think Make Live Youth

Edward Julian exemplifies what it means to turn adversity into a powerful platform for change. His life story, grounded in resilience and determination, speaks directly to those looking for a way forward, offering a blueprint for hope and transformation.

— Dr. Laura Espy-Bell
Physician and Advocate

When I asked the Mayor of Columbus, Ohio, to join me in recruiting committed adult men for a Summer Reading Program for Young Men, he agreed. However, when I asked men from the community to volunteer, few stepped up. One of the few was Mr. Edward Julian, who came with his program.

He was committed to sharing his personal experiences of growing up in Cleveland, Ohio. He did not hesitate to be transparent about the mistakes he made and his desire to ensure these young boys did not follow the same path. Mr. Julian was always mindful of the mental and emotional state of the young men, whether they were 12, 14, or 18 years old. The program drew participants of many ages and academic abilities, and Mr. Julian was able to connect with all of them.

He also shared his program Begin, Believe, Become, which quickly became the theme of our sessions. The young men gravitated toward it, and we referenced it each time we met because Mr. Julian made it relevant to their lives.

— **Mrs. Hanifah Kambon**
Educator

Edward Julian is literally a walking testimony. His story is one of dreams deferred but never denied. From a place of humility, transparency, and love, Edward shares his journey of self-actualization, which is sure to be an inspiration!

— **India Wilson, M.Ed.**
Principal & STEM Pundit

My association with Edward A. Julian, Sr began in June when he was our featured guest on RADIO OPAC (Ohio Prison Arts Connection), speaking about his work as a spoken word artist and his motivational talks in the prison system.

I also attended a rally he led in Gahanna to lift up our city in connection with Black Lives Matter. His radio appearance, stage presence, and his use of positive language to bring people together impressed me greatly.

— Patricia Wynn Brown Writer & Performer, Columbus, Ohio

edwardajuliansr.com

"This book is more than a story. It is a roadmap." Judge
James E. Green

From Inmate to Advocate:
A Journey of
Transformation

Edward A. Julian, Sr.

The Begin Within Initiative, LLC

Edited by Anne Mercer Larson

✉ Email: beginbelievebecome14@gmail.com

Website: www.edwardajuliansr.com

ISBN: 979-8-9989900-0-7 (Softcover)

ISBN: 979-8-9989900-2-1 (Hardcover)

Cover design by Toiana Tucker

www.toituckerphotography.com

Important Facts Disclaimer

The Important Facts listed at the end of each chapter include the website they came from for the reader to use to further explore the issues. They are not listed as specific citations in academic format.

Table of Contents

*Note: All poems are by the author, Edward A. Julian, Sr

Foreword

━━━◇◇◆◇◇◆◇◇◆◇◇◆◇◇◆◇◇◆◇◇◆◇◇━━━

It is with profound respect and deep admiration that I write this for Edward Julian. I first met him shortly after his release from prison, and before officiating his marriage. From the very beginning, three things about Edward struck me with undeniable force.

First, his unwavering determination to never return to prison. Second, his steadfast commitment to Giena and their family, including her three daughters, whom Edward embraced as his own. And third, his relentless drive to prevent others from facing the same fate he once endured, helping those who have been incarcerated find a way forward without falling back into the system.

As a judge with over three decades on the bench, I have witnessed countless individuals pass through the revolving door of our justice system. Yet, Edward has ignited in me a renewed sense of purpose, a commitment to not only administering justice but also to ensuring that those who encounter the justice system have the tools and opportunities they need to avoid returning to it.

This book is more than a story. It is a roadmap. It will serve as an essential tool for criminal justice professionals. More importantly, it is a tool for those who are at risk of incarceration, are currently incarcerated, or are navigating life after release. It is a testament to resilience, hope, and the possibility of real change.

Congratulations, Edward, on this extraordinary work and for your unwavering dedication to helping others forge a better path.

Judge James E. Green, Franklin County Municipal Court Columbus Ohio

GROWTH AND TRANSFORMATION

Life is complicated
Stress is a distraction
Words like bullets
Piercing through my Black skin

I'm not good at giving negative feedback
Pointing out the flaws of others
I'm not good at treating you like an enemy
When I see you as my brother

I suffer from introvert anxiety
I suffer from mental abuse delivered by society
I suffered silently through my teenage years
Pretending to be strong, hiding all my fears
Another mistaken identity
I carry post-disloyalty syndrome silently

Growing up in the '70s, life wasn't easy
Especially when broke felt like a daily identity

Not knowing how to read was its own kind of fight

Stumbling through words, chasing the light

Nobody cares about the weight I bear

Endless possibilities led straight to prison daycare

Nightmares haunt my humanity

A bird in one hand is worth more than fantasy

A blunt in my other hand, inhale, exhale

I push forward through this broken insanity

"Life, liberty, and the pursuit of happiness." Just words

In the hood, it's betrayal, backstabbing, and dreams deferred

Small joys in being home

Big dreams drowned in three shots of Patron

Still, I chase a learned misguided reality

Searching for a way out

Or am I just the product of my environment's unspoken formality?

The joy of waking next to my wife

Her imperturbable presence balances my life

God grant me the serenity to change the things

I still witness at night

Preface

Transformation is rarely a single event. It's an ongoing, often grueling journey of facing yourself, confronting your past, and owning your choices. When I first entered prison, I was overwhelmed with disappointment and hurt. I blamed the person who snitched on me, the teacher who kept me from graduating, my brother for introducing me to the streets, and my basketball coach for not supporting me. At first, all I could think about was how others had wronged me. But as time passed, I began to ask myself: Why was I letting someone else control my future? Why was I allowing their actions to dictate my destiny?

As the years went by, I realized I wasn't just a victim of betrayal, I was a victim of my own choices. Until I owned them, I would remain stuck.

Forgiveness became less about others and more about freeing myself from the bitterness holding me captive.

Five years into my sentence, I experienced a turning point. During a visit, my son asked me to take him to the vending machine, not understanding why I couldn't. A yellow line on the floor separated us, a symbol of everything I had lost. That day, I cried and prayed, vowing never to let anyone or anything put me in that position again. It didn't change everything overnight, but it was the first step toward reclaiming my life.

Prison wasn't just a place of punishment; it became the forge for my transformation. I started teaching fitness classes, devouring self-help courses, and writing eight books and over 300 poems. I learned that if I wanted others to invest in me, I had to invest in myself. Forgiveness wasn't just about healing; it was the beginning of my journey of transformation.

When I was released in 2012, I moved back to Cleveland to live with my mother. I took any job that came my way, working at a homeless shelter in the winter and landscaping in the summer. Eventually I secured a job at US Foods, gaining stability and rebuilding my life. Then I met Giena. She had just come out of a 14-year marriage, and I had just finished 14 years in prison. Together, we found strength in our shared struggles, building a new life for her daughters and my son and daughter.

Life has a way of coming full circle. I never imagined I would return to prison, not as a prisoner, but as someone offering light in the darkest of places. Walking back into those same halls, no longer bound but standing as a mentor and guide, speaks to the incredible power of transformation. What once held me back now stands as a reminder of how far I've risen.

What started as a personal mission has grown into a commitment to helping others break free, not just from incarceration, but from any struggle, pain, or circumstance that keeps them from living fully. Whether it's fear, doubt, or the weight of the past, this journey is about showing that transformation is possible for everyone. This book isn't just about my journey. It's a testament to the possibilities that exist for anyone willing to embrace change.

Dedication

To My Wife, Giena

When I think of everything we've been through, one memory that burns brightest in my mind is the time you saved my life. For a week at home, I was trapped in a body that betrayed me. Unable to eat, unable to sleep, with pain that felt like a weight pulling me under. Each hour stretched endlessly, as if life itself was slipping away. But even in those dark times, you stood by me, unwavering, refusing to let me fade. You fought for me when I couldn't fight for myself, and when I was ready to give in, you made sure I got the help I needed.

For the next 13 days in the hospital, you never left. Not for a single second. Day and night, you stayed, sleeping beside me in the bed or on the couch, wherever you could. You were my strength when I had none. You challenged the doctors, asked all the right questions, and never accepted anything less than the best care. You were relentless. But you were also my comfort, bringing me moments of laughter and light even when things felt impossible. It wasn't just your courage and love that saved me, it was your joy, your belief that we would get through it together.

Your smile doesn't just light up a room, it changes the atmosphere. Those pretty, tantalizing brown eyes, full of life, still draw me in just as deeply as they did the first time I saw you. There's a gravity about you, a warmth that people can't help but be pulled toward. It's not just your beauty on the outside that captivates, it's the kindness, strength, and unwavering spirit inside you that makes everyone feel seen, valued, and loved. You bring light wherever you go, and the world feels brighter with you in it.

Those 13 days are only a piece of our story. They reflect the 13 years we've shared since I came home. Through every struggle, every victory, and every beautiful, joyful moment, you've been by my side. You've celebrated with me, lifted me up when I was down, and given me the strength to keep pushing forward. When I had nothing—no money, no strength, no hope—you gave me everything. You reminded me how to laugh, how to dream, and how to live.

This book is for you, Giena. You are my greatest blessing, my protector, my joy, my strength, and the most beautiful soul I have ever known. Without you, none of this would exist. You saved me, not just once, but again and again, so I will forever be thankful for you, and the life we continue to build together, filled with love and laughter, wrapped with an unbreakable bond.

Acknowledgments

To my mother—Momma, you stood by me through 14 years of incarceration. You never wavered, never gave up on me, and always believed in my potential. You carried me through the hardest moments of my life, and I couldn't have done it without you.

To my wife, Giena Julian—it feels as though God passed me from my mother's care into your arms. You have been my balance, my wisdom, and my strength. After walking through your own 14-year journey, you've stood by me, through the ups and downs. Your trust and unwavering love have been my rock. You guided me when I was lost, and you believed in me even when I struggled to believe in myself. I couldn't have made it this far without you by my side.

To my son Edward and my daughter Payton—our journey together has not been without its challenges, but through it all, you've been the reason I continue to push forward. Every step I take is fueled by my desire to create a better future for us. No matter the distance or difficulties, my love and commitment to you are unshakable, and I will never stop working toward the bond we deserve.

To my daughters Selene and Seleste, who were 3 years old, and Sydney, who was 5 years old when I met them. The same ages as my son and daughter when I went away to prison. Our connection was nothing short of divine. It felt like a second chance to be the father I couldn't be before. You started calling me "Pops," and soon, everyone followed. You've brought a new light into my life, and I am forever grateful for the joy and purpose you've given me.

To Judge James Green—thank you for the light and direction you offered me when I needed it most. You not only provided marriage counseling to Giena and me, but you also opened the doors of your courtroom, allowing me to see the path forward in a new way. Your guidance and belief in my potential gave me strength, and I carry that impact with me daily. Thank you for seeing beyond my past and helping me build my future.

To my friend and lawyer Carlos Crawford, Chief Public Defender, Delaware County, Ohio—your relentless dedication and tireless efforts to have my felonies expunged have given me a fresh start in life. I am forever grateful for your support and friendship.

To Dr. Laura Epsy-Bell—during a time of sickness, you helped save my life, and you did it alongside Giena. I owe you both a debt of gratitude that words cannot fully express.

To Deshaun Donaldson—thank you for being the bridge that connected me to India. Your belief in my potential and your support at the start of my journey gave me the confidence to share my voice. That introduction was more than an opportunity; it was a stepping stone that has been instrumental in my growth.

To India Wilson, M.Ed.—thank you for not only giving me a platform at Baldwin Road Junior High in Reynoldsburg, Ohio, but for truly believing in the power of my story and my poetry. Your willingness to provide me with a space to inspire others has had a profound impact, and I am forever grateful for the trust and encouragement you've shown me.

To the companies that shaped my journey—MCS T.O.U.C.H. (Teaching Opportunity Unity by Connecting Hearts), where I was first given the chance to facilitate groups inside four different prisons in Ohio. This opportunity helped me discover my passion for working with others. The eyeglasses and contact lens industry, where I built a career and was honored to be selected for the Committee of Diversity, Equity, and Inclusion. What made that moment significant was being the only member without a formal title, surrounded by managers and district managers. Yet, I was given a voice among leaders, an honor that I carried with me throughout my career.

Now, at Think Make Live Youth, as a Credible Messenger, I have the privilege of using my experiences to help others rebuild their lives. A credible messenger is a trusted mentor who connects with youth, guiding them through challenges and helping them build confidence and self-awareness.

Through weekly group sessions, they create a safe space for young people to explore issues and make positive choices for a better future. In addition to my work with youth, I also serve as a Group Mentor & Facilitator, supporting men and women as they navigate the challenges of reentry that I once faced myself.

Lastly, being recognized by the U.S. Probation Department as one of the most successful restored citizens has been both humbling and motivating. It reminds me of the power of transformation and the potential we all have to rebuild our lives, no matter where we've come from.

Special Acknowledgments

To Donna Grill—thank you for being the kind of public defender who truly changes lives. Your dedication, compassion, and belief in your clients makes all the difference and I am honored to acknowledge the role you played in my journey.

After exhausting every legal avenue and spending over $100,000 on attorneys who wouldn't even visit me, I turned to the court-appointed lawyer system as my only remaining option. That's when you stepped in. Unlike the others, you took the time to hear my story, visit me in person, and fight tirelessly to bring my case back to court.

Because of your efforts, I received a sentence reduction and the opportunity to return home and rebuild my life. Your advocacy gave me more than a second chance; it gave me the ability to reclaim my purpose and move forward. Thank you, Donna, for standing by me when it mattered most. Your determination and professionalism will always be remembered with gratitude.

To Anne Mercer Larson, M.O.B.—you have worn many hats in this process of writing my manuscript and navigating life's challenges: Creative Consultant, Manuscript Advisor, Content Advisor, Editorial Consultant.

Since 2015, you've been the driving force behind the scenes—even though we've never met in person. You've been right there, helping me shape, not only this book, but also my voice, offering your insights, encouragement, editing, guidance, and belief in my story when I needed it most.

Every suggestion and every word of advice has been a gift that has made *From Inmate to Advocate: A Journey of Transformation* stronger and more authentic. I can't thank you enough for your friendship and unwavering dedication. You've been a lifeline in ways that go far beyond this book. Thank you, Anne—you are truly part of this journey with me.

Introduction

Throughout history, people have made choices driven by personal needs, shaped by the circumstances around them.

When it comes to prisons, the narratives society accepts often fall short of capturing the full truth. These limited perspectives fail to reveal the complexity, the cost, and the real stories of those behind bars. This book is not just about unveiling what happens in the shadows, it's about unlocking the truth, sharing experiences, and exploring the power of transformation.

After serving 14 years in prison, I know firsthand how public perceptions and policies can shape the lives of those behind bars and the families they leave behind. While incarcerated, I made a choice not to let society's limitations define my future. Instead, I developed new habits, embraced new ways of thinking, and redefined my path forward. That transformation didn't stop when I walked out of prison. It became the foundation for my commitment to helping others navigate the same system I once endured by advocating for meaningful change in how we approach justice.

Today, I stand as a living testament to transformation and growth, a voice for change, and a proud advocate for the philosophy I developed that saved me: *Begin, Believe, Become.* But make no mistake, prison changes you. Inside those walls, you are tested every day. The burden doesn't just fall on the incarcerated; it's carried by families, communities, and society as a whole.

This book sheds light on the hidden costs, the untold stories, and the realities behind those gates, challenging the narratives we've been conditioned to accept. Their sacrifices inspired me to advocate for a system that doesn't just warehouse people but addresses the root causes of incarceration. These experiences shaped my mission to not only rebuild my life but to help others do the same.

One belief often taken at face value is that prison serves the greater good of society. But at what cost? It costs $36,000 to

$44,000 each year, about $100 to $120 a day to incarcerate someone in the U.S. Yet only a fraction of that goes toward rehabilitation or reentry support, leaving taxpayers funding containment instead of true correction.

Still, that figure doesn't account for the financial and emotional burden placed on families, who must step in to provide for essentials like food, hygiene products, and other basic needs when prison provisions fall short. Their commitment made me reflect on the larger societal cost of incarceration; the missed opportunities to address poverty, mental health, and education, the very issues that could prevent incarceration in the first place.

While prisoners may earn a few cents an hour working in programs like U.N.I.C.O.R. (Federal Prison Industries, Inc.), dismantling e-waste for pennies on the dollar or simply enduring the everyday grind of incarceration, the emotional and financial burden extends far beyond the prison walls.

Families drive for hours, paying for tolls and buying gas, just to share a fleeting visit. And when leaving, they carry the heavy weight of knowing their loved one remains behind bars, caught in a system that feels unyielding.

Prison is a place where people from all walks of life converge, and through that diversity, I learned more than I ever expected. It became a cultural exchange, where I met men from Puerto Rico, Mexico, Jamaica, and all over the world. We shared stories, traditions, and food. I learned how to make Mexican and Jamaican dishes that I never would have experienced otherwise. On holidays like Thanksgiving, we'd pool our commissary food to create meals that reminded us of home. For a few hours, we weren't inmates, we were just people, connecting through shared culture.

And then there was football. Sundays were sacred. The rivalry between Browns and Ravens fans got heated, but it wasn't money we were betting, it was pride. Losers had to dance for the crowd, and the sight of a grown man trying to moonwalk in shower slides was priceless. Those moments of humor and humanity broke through the monotony, reminding us all of who we were before incarceration.

This book confronts long-held beliefs: that prison provides safety, that it reforms and rehabilitates, and that the criminal justice system delivers fairness. Together, we'll examine these narratives, explore their origins, and uncover the truth behind them. After each chapter, you'll find a poem that captures not only my experiences, but also the voices of countless others who have endured the system. What I learned behind bars and through reentry is that transformation isn't just personal, it's collective. The work to shift narratives and dismantle systemic barriers is a journey we must take together.

The truth is, these beliefs serve only those who benefit from keeping reality hidden. While reading, I encourage you to question everything you think you know about incarceration and reentry. The statistics, the personal stories, and the cultural exchanges shared here, aim to reveal what truly happens behind those walls and in the lives forever shaped by incarceration.

This is more than a book; it's a call to action. It's an invitation to look beyond the surface, to seek a deeper understanding, and to ignite real change. Now, let's unlock the truth and embark on this journey together.

The Heart of a Man

The heart of a man, stuck in a situation
To live is to die... what's your occupation?
I've done all I can, lost all patience
Fighting silent battles, learning hard lessons

Moving beyond circumstance
In prison, still taking prison chances
Dreams deferred, yet hope still dances
Trying to break free from life's harsh advances

Clouded by indecision
Grasping for freedom
Bound by a 20-year sentence

The heart of a man, caught in a sea of emotion
The essence of America drowning in a rising tide of broken choices
Companies gone, "Black jobs" shipped offshore

Modern-day plantations scrub prison floors
Slave labor making millions for UNICOR
Brenda got a baby
While healthcare no longer for the poor

This is the reality of crushed expectations
Where society breeds both hope and desperation
400 years… no true liberation
Still stuck in a zone… what's your aspiration?

Think before you speak
It's easier to build strong children
Than repair broken men at their peak
Your life is God's gift to the world
So what's your gift to God?

From inmate to advocate
What a journey to trod
A life transformed, no longer the same
A testimony of growth, embracing the chan

CHAPTER 1

The Cost of My Choices:
The Hustle, The Illusion, The Truth

I wasn't just selling drugs. I was selling destruction. I used to tell myself I wasn't just making a living but doing what I had to do. I wasn't forcing anyone to use drugs, just giving people what they wanted. And in a world where real opportunities seemed out of reach, making fast money seemed like the only choice.

Looking back, I was feeding the same system that was designed to destroy us, selling drugs to my own people.

When I started, I had no idea what that life would eventually become. There were no killings, no robberies tied to it, just fast money. Crack cocaine had just hit the scene, and I did not see the damage at first. I came from a working-class neighborhood, a place where people held jobs and took care of their families. My mother was one of them.

Growing up, drugs was not the focus, competition was. It was all about school rivalries, sports, and childhood games. We spent our days playing hide-and-go-seek, kickball, and dodgeball. The biggest arguments weren't over money; instead they were over who had the best jump shot, who was the fastest, or which school had the best football or basketball team. By the time I reached my senior year, though, everything started to shift.

The same guys I battled on the basketball court, the same ones I fought with over school pride, were not rivals anymore. Suddenly, we were all on the same team, but the game wasn't sports. We went from fouling each other hard on the basketball court to exchanging money and drugs in alleyways and parking lots. One day, we were just kids with dreams; the next, players in a game we never even realized we'd been drafted into.

People talk about opportunity like it's something everyone has, but in my neighborhood, opportunity was limited. By the time crack cocaine hit, the choices were clear: hustle, deal, or be broke. That was it. That was the reality.

I didn't grow up seeing CEOs, doctors, lawyers, or pharmaceutical reps. Those careers did not feel real because they were not part of my world. I wasn't exposed to them. And exposure means everything. If you don't see something, how do you know it's possible? Instead, the only people I saw with real money were hustlers and drug dealers. They were the ones with the cars, the jewelry, the respect, they had it all. In my neighborhood, that looked like success.

I swore, I would never work like my mother did, 14-hours a day, 7 days a week. She worked tirelessly and took pride in keeping a clean home, all while raising us the right way. What we had, she made look good. Still, I hated seeing her work that hard. I hated that she could not make it to my basketball games because she carried the burden of providing for 10 children, 5 boys and 5 girls. I chose a different path; one that, at the time, felt like the only real option.

Before I realized it, my community became unrecognizable. What used to be a working-class neighborhood built on paychecks and pride was overtaken by the rise of crack cocaine and the chaos it brought with it. The same women I once looked up to, the ones I thought were beautiful and carried themselves with grace, were now selling their bodies for crack cocaine.

The same men I saw working hard, providing for their families, and raising their kids, became addicts, doing whatever they could to get a hit. Men could not sell their bodies like women could, so they found other ways. They washed cars for drug dealers, cut grass, and cleaned windows; grown men, once strong, now reduced to begging for the next high.

Then came the moment that changed everything.

During Christmas time, a woman, desperate for crack cocaine, offered to sell me her body along with her kids' toys.

Instead, I gave her what she wanted. Still, she kept coming back. Finally, I bought the toys, not because I needed them, but because I knew I had to give them back. On Christmas day, I returned them to her house, giving her kids a chance to have something under the tree.

That sad moment stuck with me. No matter how I tried to justify it, I was the reason she was in that position. It was the day I could no longer ignore the destructive activities I was a part of.

At the time, my friends and I thought we were getting ahead and breaking the cycle of poverty. We paid for college tuition. We started small businesses. We bought houses for our mothers, wives, girlfriends, and side chicks. In our eyes, we weren't just making fast money, we were building something, creating a way out.

Unfortunately, it was a lie. If selling drugs was really a way out, why did it destroy so many lives? And the million-dollar question: How did crack cocaine hit all 50 states simultaneously? We didn't own boats. We didn't own planes. We weren't flying shipments across borders. We barely had cars to drive. So how the hell did this drug get into our communities? The answer was right in front of me. It was never an accident. It was a set up.

Crack cocaine did not just appear in Black and low-income neighborhoods. It was orchestrated by a system that looked the other way. Even government reports later revealed that during the 1980s, officials knew some U.S.-backed groups were connected to drug trafficking, but enforcement was ignored when politics took priority. Those decisions hit our communities the hardest. Factories closed, opportunities disappeared, and drugs filled the empty spaces left behind. By the time we realized what crack was really doing, families were torn apart, the arrests started, and the cycle was in motion.

Then came the laws that punished us instead of protecting us. The 1986 Anti-Drug Abuse Act created a 100-to-1 sentencing disparity between crack and powder cocaine, devastating families and flooding prisons with Black men and women. The drugs may not have been planted, but the conditions were.

Prison didn't just give me time to think, it gave me the chance to see the bigger picture. I met men from all 50 states and although we didn't know each other, we lived similar lives, made the same choices, and ended up in the same place.

When I first started selling drugs, I thought I was chasing survival. I didn't realize I was recruiting, and building a blueprint others would follow.

I started hearing about all the younger dudes, moving up the ranks, picking up where I left off. One person in particular stands out, he sat back and observed as if he was studying for a test. Every move I made was permission for him to do the same.

Years later, while incarcerated, I heard about him, flashy, loud, moving weight. He bought cars, jewelry, and other luxuries. Not the same kind but chasing the same dream. However, he wasn't the only one. He was just the one everybody talked about, he was getting the most money. He wanted out but didn't know how.

The trap of selling drugs isn't just about the money, it's an addiction; the fast life, the power, the illusion of control. It's a high of its own. And once you're in, it's hard to break free.

Today, he is locked up, caught with $9.5 million worth of crack cocaine and fentanyl. Unfortunately, my influence had stretched further than I ever imagined.

When I came home, I saw something that shook me to my core. The younger guys from my neighborhood, the ones who had been 12, 13, 14 when I left, greeted me with praise. They weren't praising the man I had become. They were praising the man I used to be, and I was ashamed.

I once swore I'd never work like my mother did, 7 days a week, 14 hour shifts. But after my release, I found myself doing exactly that. For twelve years, I worked seven days a week, 14 hours a day, just like my mother. The very thing I ran from became my reality.

That's when I knew I couldn't change my past, but I could change my purpose. And in the end, the price you pay is always greater than the money you earn.

Important Facts:

- Racial Disparities in Incarceration:

  By the early 1990s, over 80% of those sentenced for crack offenses were Black, despite research showing most crack users were white.

  bjs.ojp.gov

  aclu.org

- Government Awareness:

  Declassified reports confirmed U.S. officials were aware of cocaine trafficking by Contra-linked groups in the 1980s but failed to intervene.

  cia.gov

- Economic Collapse in Urban Communities:
  Job losses, redlining, and lack of investment in Black neighborhoods during the 1980s created the perfect conditions for drugs to take root.

  brookings.edu

  nul.org

10/5: THE CODE WE LIVE BY

I stand 10 toes down, 5 fingers balled up just to give you a pound
10/5 is my stomping ground for all you lame and clowns
Be aware when you come around my part of town

We don't mean-mug
We just grew up with a frown
Y'all puppies, we are the real dog pound...

Shh, Relax and Breathe Easy
Don't make a sound
10 shots, 5 bodies lying on the ground

I'm just a product of my environment
A product of my own entitlements
If you asked my mom, she'll tell you I'm heaven sent
If you ask my dad, I'm George Clinton, Funkadelic Parliament

My hood say I should run for president

I'm too busy dodging cases but the block knows I'm relevant

Disrespect me, you closing doors apologies can't reopen

Disrespect me, it's an unspoken friendship broken

Don't confuse movement with motion

You running in place

I Have A Dream

You continue to use unwanted slogan

Jump shot like Steve Logan

Step back, Dame Dolla, potent

Polariscope, blurry vision internal stress doesn't mix

Trapped in the game

Kaleidoscope, no easy fix

CHAPTER 2

The Thin Line Between Justice and Judgment: Society's Choice

The guard's hands moved over me, checking every pocket and seam, before waving me through the metal detector. "Take off your boots," he ordered, nodding at the steel-toed footwear we were required to wear in the UNICOR factory.

I slipped them off and watched as he banged them against the ground, checking for anything hidden inside. The sound echoed sharply in the small hallway, a reminder of the restrictions forced upon me, the pain of confinement, the anger of being stripped of my dignity, and the frustration of knowing how far I'd fallen from the life I once knew.

Once I cleared the metal detector, I slipped the boots back on and stepped into the factory with a few other guys starting that day. We were the new labor, handed over to a system that didn't care about our past or future.

An inmate walked over to us, his movements casual but quick. He nodded and said, "What's up?" His tone was relaxed, but his eyes darted around the room. The conversation started with the usual questions: "Where are you from? What unit are you in? How much time did you get?" It was small talk, nothing deep. Just as one of the guys was answering, a commotion broke out about ten feet away.

Two inmates were arguing, their voices low but intense. Before anyone could intervene, one of them threw a hot cup of coffee he was holding into the other man's face. Quickly, he jumped on the long wooden table used to place the items we worked on in the warehouse, and kicked the guy in the face as he sat in a chair at his workstation.

For a moment, everything froze. The machines, the voices, even the air felt still. But the only thing that didn't stop was the blood, pouring from his nose like water rushing downstream. Then, just as quickly, everything went back to normal. The guards escorted the attacker away in handcuffs, and the other man was taken to the infirmary. Men turned away, guards went back to their posts, and the work continued. It was like nothing happened.

The inmate walked over to us and said, "Welcome to UNICOR." I stood there, trying to process what I'd just seen. It was my first day, and already I understood this place wasn't just about work. It was about staying ready at all times.

UNICOR, the trade name for Federal Prison Industries (FPI), was established by Congress in 1934. Its mission, according to the government, was to protect society and reduce crime by preparing inmates for successful reentry through job training. But for those of us working there, it didn't feel like preparation. It felt like exploitation.

The system wasn't designed to reward hard work; it was designed to generate profit, turning cheap labor into revenue.

The signs we made were sold at a profit far beyond the pennies we earned to produce them. Some men saved their paychecks for months just to send a few dollars home to their families or to buy handcrafted items like jewelry boxes, carved nameplates, or custom shirts to send as gifts.

I tried to convince myself it was enough—enough to justify the hours spent working in UNICOR, enough to feel like I was accomplishing something. Yet, it never was. I felt hollow, like I was working without progressing toward anything meaningful, learning nothing of real value.

In UNICOR, the day was often like an endless loop of routine: clear the metal detector, lace up the boots, sit at the workstation. But it wasn't the work that defined those hours, it was the conversations. We talked about where we came from and how so many of us shared the same story. No father in the home, and a struggling mother raising too many kids, with too few resources. In financially starved neighborhoods, crack was introduced like a trap, and as young men, we saw the chance to make money we'd never had before. It didn't matter whether it was illegal or wrong.

When you've had nothing, survival outweighs the consequences. Selling drugs or using them was part of the same cycle, feeding a system that thrived on our desperation. As we pieced together our stories in those conversations, one truth became clear. We weren't in prison by chance, we'd been set up from the start.

I told myself to focus on the silver lining. For me, the silver lining was going home. Every day presented the same routine: counting hours, days, and eventually years to reach that silver lining. So, going home was the goal, which meant doing everything in my power to get there. Also, it meant doing everything in my power to provide for my son and daughter with what little I had.

The reality of what we earned was impossible to ignore. The pay was a constant reminder of how little value the system placed on our time and labor. Here's how the pay was structured:

- Grade 1: $1.15 per hour
- Grade 2: $0.92 per hour
- Grade 3: $0.69 per hour
- Grade 4: $0.46 per hour

- Grade 5: $0.23 per hour

Most federal inmates, however, worked under a different pay scale, earning between $10 and $25 per month, with the lower end of this scale being far more common. The Inmate Performance Pay Grade Scale was as follows:

- Grade 1: $0.40 per hour
- Grade 2: $0.29 per hour
- Grade 3: $0.17 per hour
- Grade 4: $0.12 per hour
- Maintenance Pay: $5.25 per month

Advancing beyond Grade 4 required a GED or high school diploma, something many men inside didn't have. Even with my Associate of Arts degree and nearly completing my bachelor's, I stayed stuck at Grade 4 for months, until I went to the SHU (Special Housing Unit) for a fight with a guy from New York.

We were in the dayroom, watching basketball. I sat in the only open seat available to watch the game. In prison, you claim your chair and it's yours, depending on where you're from, how many homies you have on the compound, how long you've been in the unit, or how willing you are to fight to prove you're not someone to mess with.

After about seven months of being locked up, I knew the rules, but I wasn't willing to be viewed as soft or let anyone take advantage of me. That day, I was sitting in a chair I knew wasn't mine. It belonged to someone else, but it was an open seat, so I sat down. I knew the guy who usually sat there, and he didn't seem to mind.

A guy called Black from New York walked in, he didn't have to say a word, his presence alone was enough to command attention. He stood over another man sitting in "his" chair, and without hesitation, the guy moved.

I didn't plan to stay in the TV room long because I had a phone call to make. Plus, I quickly learned how easily a simple debate about a game or a foul call could escalate into a full-blown fight. I had just pushed back my chair to leave when—bam!—a fist came out of nowhere. My head snapped, lights bursting in front of my eyes like fireworks. Time seemed to drag as I stumbled forward, reaching blindly until my hands locked onto him. We scuffled and tussled, crashing into chairs and bodies, each desperate for control. Shouts filled the air, but all I heard was the thundering of my own heartbeat, until suddenly arms from every side tore us apart.

Still in a daze from the blow, looking around, I noticed several men from all states and men from New York rushing toward the TV room. My homeboy, who was my celly (cellmate), and his friend from New York pulled me out of the TV room, and walked me into his room, while questioning me about what happened with Black.

"He sucker-punched me," was all I could come up with.

"Black need to stop this shit, man," said the guy from New York.

My lip was swollen and my pride was shattered. I had a decision to make. Should I suck it up and move on, or grab a knife and plan my revenge? I was in a no-win situation, and if it hadn't been for my celly stepping in and using his influence, the outcome would have been different. I knew I was outnumbered and the odds weren't in my favor. The smart move was to let it go.

Rumors traveled fast, and word came for me to meet at the gym after count. The OG who sent the message had been locked up for over a decade, moving through several institutions and earning respect along the way. Later that day, the eight homeboys we had on the compound gathered at the gym. His main concern was how I felt I handled the situation and whether I wanted a fair fight. "If you want to get a fair one, just know Black keeps a blade under his tongue," he warned. New York men were known for keeping a razor blade in their mouth, under their tongue, then spitting it out in an instant to use as a weapon. He leaned closer. "If you want, I can just give you a knife. You know what you gotta do."

I was trying to go home. That meant doing whatever it took to stay on track, swallowing my pride and walking away from a fight I didn't start. So, I told him I was cool. "I stood my ground," I said, trying to convince myself as much as him. It wasn't about winning or losing. It was about keeping my focus, staying alive, and making it to the day I could leave prison behind.

With my lip tucked into my mouth, I tried to hide the swelling, hoping no one would notice I'd been in a fight. The next day, during a basketball game, a foul was called after I went up for a rebound. I fell to the ground, holding my mouth and asking, "Is it bleeding? Is it swollen?" Putting on my best act, I walked over to the officer, showed him my lip, and told him the guy who fouled me, elbowed me in the mouth. It seemed like a good enough excuse.

Later that day, after leaving the game and heading back to the unit, the guards came for me and Black. Without much explanation, we were taken to the hole under investigation. The hole was an isolated place of punishment, a test of your mental and emotional strength.

The 30 days in isolation was suffocating, each day feeling longer than the last. When we were finally released, something unexpected happened. Black, who was on his way to be transferred to a lower-security prison closer to his family, came up to me. For whatever reason, he thanked me for not telling the truth, for not snitching on him. His thanks didn't bring closure to my feelings. I did what I had to do for me and my safety.

Looking back, it was definitely a no-win situation for me. I had to do what was necessary to defend myself and fight for my future. There was no other option.

When I was transferred to Federal Correctional Institute Elkton, Ohio, I knew what UNICOR really meant. There, the work shifted to recycling old electronics, breaking down computers, TVs, and other equipment filled with toxic chemicals like lead and mercury. Men from UNICOR would return to the unit after finishing those shifts with their boots leaving trails of fine dust behind. The smell of metal clung to their clothes, and the dust spread across the floors, into the washing machines, and into the air we all breathed.

At that point, it wasn't about the low wages anymore—it was a fight for respect and dignity. A few extra cents an hour wasn't worth risking my health, even if it meant sending a little more money home or buying something small for my kids. In the end, it became a test of my manhood.

When I refused to work under those conditions, the punishments came swiftly. I lost visitation rights, my commissary privileges were cut, I was moved from a larger two-man room to a cramped three-man cubicle on the top bunk, and I was threatened with being sent to the SHU (Special Housing Unit). My case manager even demanded I pay $250 a month toward my $5,000 fine, basing that amount on how much money my family and friends sent me. My fine did not have a time limit, but that didn't matter to them. The prison made it clear non-compliance wasn't an option.

The system was focused on extracting every dollar possible, no matter how it affected an inmate's ability to survive.

This wasn't about rehabilitation or preparing you for release. It wasn't enough to serve your time. You had to fight every day for survival both physically and mentally. In addition to personal battles, and family battles. The ongoing stress was overwhelming to say the least.

There comes a time when you must stand up for what you believe in and refuse to let the system, your case manager, or the guards take what little dignity, respect, and manhood you have left. For me, it wasn't just about surviving. It was about holding on to who I was and proving that no one could take that from me.

I took a job cleaning the housing unit and found other ways to hustle. My shifts were spent scrubbing floors, mopping up the trails of dust left behind, and wiping down washing machines that could not adequately clean the clothes contaminated with toxic chemicals.

Beyond my assigned job, I hustled in every way I could. Hustling was a way of life in prison. Everyone had one. If you worked in the kitchen, you could smuggle food back to the unit to sell. Guys in the laundry would sneak out extra clothes or blankets for a price. Those working in the hospital could swipe alcohol pads, which were valuable for keeping your face or hands clean. Even in the captain's office, there was a hustle. Items confiscated from inmates such as radios, extra pairs of tennis shoes, or clothing, would be stolen and taken back to the compound or units to be sold. In the law library, the "jailhouse lawyers" hustled by helping men file their briefs and appeals, charging a fee for their "legal" expertise.

Men working in landscaping or plumbing also found ways to hustle. Landscaping and plumbing crews had access to steel tools, which could be fashioned into a shank—a knife in prison slang.

Those working in UNICOR had another kind of hustle. While breaking down electronics, they had access to cords, which were taken back to the unit and used to make "stingers." A stinger is a makeshift device that works like a hot plate; inmates would plug the exposed cord into an outlet and drop the heated end into water, causing it to boil. The boiling water could then be used to heat or cook food. To cook this way, you'd tie your food in plastic bags, double-wrapped to keep the water out, and immerse it in the boiling water until done. It wasn't just about money at all. It was survival – a fragile attempt to claim control in a place designed to strip it away.

I organized fitness classes for guys who wanted to lose weight or get in shape, charging for my time and expertise. I coached others on improving their fitness routines, creating a small but steady stream of income.

At one point during my incarceration, I made a decision that could have cost me everything. In a place where opportunity was scarce and temptation was everywhere, I convinced myself that taking a shortcut would somehow make things easier.

I got involved in a hustle, something that, at the time, seemed calculated and low-risk.

It involved timing, trust, and precision. A system of discreet exchanges and carefully planned movements that had to go unnoticed.

There was a method to smuggle marijuana: every move in the visiting room had to look ordinary while staying hydrated, planning every step, and preparing for the distribution. In that moment, it felt like a survival tactic, a way to create opportunity where there was none.

But deep down I knew better. I knew the risk was far greater than the reward. I could have justified it like so many others did. I could have told myself it was just the way things were behind those walls.

But when I really sat with it, I realized this was not about survival. It was about a choice, a choice that could either strengthen the man I wanted to become, or pull me deeper into the cycle I was fighting to escape.

I made a decision that day. I would never again gamble with my future for the sake of a shortcut. The risk wasn't worth the reward, and I was not willing to bury my future by making another bad decision.

I only engaged once, testing a system that punished failure harder than it ever rewarded success. That single misstep was enough. I never tested the system twice, once was enough to show me what was at stake.

That experience didn't define me, but it did refine me. It became another brick in the foundation of the man I was determined to become.

Historical Systemic Context

When the United States was founded, the Declaration of Independence made a bold promise: that all men are created equal, with the right to life, liberty, and the pursuit of happiness.

But history tells a different story. The 13th Amendment ended slavery on paper. Yet, it included a loophole: forced labor was still allowed as punishment for a crime. That one exception became the foundation for today's system of mass incarceration.

After slavery ended, a new system called convict leasing emerged. Black Americans, newly freed, were thrown back into forced labor under false charges. Cities, states, and corporations profited while families were torn apart. Systems like cash bail and court fines only made it worse, creating endless cycles of debt and imprisonment.

In many ways, the American Dream, and American prosperity itself, was built on the foundation of a Black nightmare.

Important Facts:

- UNICOR sales in 2022: About $382 million

  www.unicor.gov

- UNICOR sales in first half of 2023: About $212.6 million

  www.unicor.gov

- Inmate wages: Between $0.23 and $1.35 per hour (Prison Policy Initiative)

  www.prisonpolicy.org

- Health hazards: Inmates in recycling are exposed to hazardous chemicals like lead, mercury, and cadmium (CDC).

  www.cdc.gov/niosh/hhe

- Psychological manipulation: Solitary confinement and loss of privileges are used as tools for compliance. www.prisonpolicy.org

- Financial impact: 80% of inmate earnings often go to fines, restitution, and other obligations. www.prisonpolicy.org

AMERICAN OR UN-AMERICAN

What constitutes American or Un-American?

Is it because I want to live decently and be civilized?

Express freedom of speech and not be penalized?

Was I Un-American for a scandal like Bill's?

The white woman screamed rape, Emmett kill

Was you an American when you stormed the Capitol

And rage turned to friction?

Overthrowing the government

Was that your mission?

Or is Un-American just a drug dealer with a conviction?

Or an immigrant, someone like you or I

A foreigner in a land, still denied a piece of the American pie

America only intended "BACK OF THE BUS"

Police brutality

"IN GOD WE TRUST"

Perpetual liars, guns full of lust

Ashes to ashes, dust to dust

I was born an American

Does that make me a citizen?

No justice under the law

Is how they belittled Black Men

Innocent until proven guilty

But whispering deceit, your gavel is filthy

Filthy with unemployment and high interest rates

Negative thinking, stripped of grace

There is no devil outside of you raising hell

The devil is you, trapped in a damn cell

Now tell

What does it profit a man to gain it all?

Let lose your soul... as America falls

The lack of love for self is our downfall

STILL I RISE, *like Maya Angelou...*

No "CAGED BIRD" to call

The same people charge us with disturbing the status quo

Lynching paved the way for our right to vote

One foot in the grave

The other foot on the side of the boat

American or Un-American. Which lie do you promote?

God is the center of my universe

You American

Living on stolen land, you journeymen

Child pornography, you old dirty men

I've been traveling on this road listening to foolish men

Committing sin after sin after sin after sin

Now that's too much power for one man

Are you American or Un-American?

CHAPTER 3

The Hidden Cost of Incarceration: Who's Accountable?

Incarceration does not just punish the person behind bars. The real cost is not the $36,000 to $44,000 the government spends annually to house an inmate. The deeper cost, the one that hits hardest, falls on families and loved ones, who silently carry the burden day after day, night after night, and year after year.

When I was locked away, time wasn't just taken from me, it was taken from my family. I missed so many moments that shaped my children's lives: their first days of school, their victories on the field, and their struggles in the classroom. I wasn't there to see them build friendships, navigate their first disagreements at school, or come running home with excitement about something new they learned.

But it wasn't just the big events that I missed. It was the quiet, everyday moments that truly left a mark like the bedtime stories, the late-night talks when they needed advice, the hugs after a tough day, and the laughter over the simplest things. I wasn't there to teach them how to stand up for themselves, help with homework, or just sit and listen when they needed me.

These are not just lost memories, but gaps in the foundation of our relationship, spaces where I should have been. No one talks about these invisible wounds, but they linger long after the sentence ends, shaping the lives of those we love in ways we will never fully understand.

The emotional toll on my family was not just about the moments lost. It was compounded by the financial weight my mom carried.

In prison, the basics are provided: a bed, a footlocker, three sets of clothes, a pair of boots, and a bar of soap. But when those supplies ran out or when hunger gnawed at me, it wasn't the prison that stepped in, it was my mother. Every extra meal I ate, every pair of socks I wore, and every bar of soap I used was paid for by my mother.

Over the course of 14 years, my mother, family, and friends sent me approximately $50,000. Roughly $15,000 was spent on phone calls to stay connected and $25,000 on hotels, renting cars, gas and food to travelto the various prisons where I did my time. My mother bore a majority of the financial and emotional toll.

The mother of my children faced her own struggles. After I was incarcerated, I had $150,000, but between paying several lawyers, buying clothes and gifts for my children, keeping up with the mortgage, and paying my truck note, the money vanished quickly. During that time, my mother helped manage what was left, sending me money, so I could buy necessities and make it through life behind bars.

But when the $150,000 ran out, everything shifted. My mother took on paying the mortgage herself, trying desperately to hold on to the house I purchased. Despite her best efforts, she eventually had to sell it. A friend of mine offered to help with the sale, but instead of giving her the full value of the equity she had rightfully earned—he kept a large portion of it for himself.

I didn't learn about this betrayal until I came home. My mother poured her heart into keeping that house, making every sacrifice to hold on to what little stability we had left, only to have her trust broken in the worst way.

No, this was not just about money. It was about holding us together when everything else seemed to be falling apart. My mother's love and determination kept us afloat in a storm that could have drowned us all.

Inside prison, survival came down to resources. Stamps, the compound's currency, played a central role in daily life and every hustle. Stamps held value like dollar bills in the free world. They could pay for just about anything such as gambling debts, drugs, food, laundry services, or even getting your clothes washed and pressed. Need legal work done? Stamps paid for that too. People traded them for favors, like loaning two books of stamps with the promise of three in return. Whether it was paying someone to cook your meals, clean your area, or help you with your appeal, stamps were the currency that made it all happen. In prison, if you had stamps, you had options, and options meant survival.

A book of stamps bought for $7 in the commissary was worth $5 in the yard, and twenty books could be sold for $100 in cash. This was often arranged by having someone's family send the money directly to my account or, in some cases, to my family. It was an underground economy that kept everything moving and turned stamps into real money.

For many, this barter system was a lifeline. But for those with limited resources, it was just another weight added to the daily grind. The hustle inside wasn't always about getting ahead, it was about making it through, one day at a time.

And just like on the outside, those with more resources controlled the system. If you did not have stamps, your options narrowed. In a place built to strip you of everything, even the smallest currency meant something.

The economic burden inside prison mirrored the financial weight my family faced outside. I scrubbed floors and cleaned units for 23 cents an hour. Over 14 years, I made $4,200, and 80% of that went straight to court fines and fees. The rest barely covered basic needs, leaving me and others constantly reaching back to our families for help.

While I was enduring these conditions inside, my family was struggling on the outside. A staggering 63% of families with incarcerated loved ones bear the financial burden, and in 83% of those cases, it's the women—mothers, wives, and sisters, who carry that load. Society often claims that women cannot lead or rise to power, but the reality proves otherwise. From running households to stepping in as providers, women have always been the backbone of families.

Moving forward, as the nation debated whether a woman could lead, I knew better. My mother led the way through every step of my life, including the years I was incarcerated and beyond.

My mom didn't just miss me, she had to rearrange her entire life around my absence. She stretched every dollar, made sacrifices to visit, and stepped in to help support my children; who grew up without my guidance, without the security of knowing that their father was there for them.

Every phone call came with a cost far greater than money. I could hear it in my children's voices: their excitement, frustration, and joy, all filtered through the distance between us. During visits I watched my children grow up before my eyes, their smiles bittersweet reminders of all the time I was missing. For them, my absence wasn't just physical, but equally emotional.

The absence of a father does not just impact a family; it ripples through entire communities. When fathers, brothers, mentors, and providers are locked away, they leave behind more than just empty beds. They leave behind responsibilities in the community—jobs, skills, and support—that go unfilled. The loss ripples outward, breaking social connections, deepening poverty, and widening inequality.

Nationally, the statistics mirror my experience. A study from the Ella Baker Center for Human Rights revealed that families of incarcerated individuals carry an average of $13,607 in court-related debt. More than one in three families went into debt just to cover phone calls and visits, and nearly two out of three reported struggling to meet basic needs such as food, housing, or medical care in order to support their loved ones in prison. The financial impact does not end once released—67% of formerly incarcerated people remain unemployed or underemployed even five years later.

As you might suspect, this impacts Black and brown families the hardest. With Black Americans incarcerated at nearly five times the rate of whites, our communities are disproportionately affected. The absence of fathers, sons, and brothers leaves communities fractured, perpetuating cycles of poverty and trauma that can take generations to heal.

During the COVID-19 pandemic, the system's deeper flaws became even more evident. Prisons were on lockdown, and visits were completely suspended. Phone calls were the only connection inmates had to the outside world, yet those calls remained a financial burden on families.

Inmates were put to work during the pandemic, manufacturing hand sanitizer, face masks, and even digging mass graves. Their labor was essential to the nation, but the pay was barely enough to call a wage. To make matters worse, health and safety were often overlooked as prisons became hotspots for the virus, causing thousands of lives lost behind bars.

While all this unfolded, I had already been home for eight years, facilitating reentry programs and providing support to those transitioning back into society. The shutdown during COVID deeply impacted my work. Facilitating groups was not just a job for me, but a form of therapy, and served as a reminder of where I have been and how far I have come. With prisons on lockdown, I could no longer go inside to lead sessions. The absence of that work left me feeling disconnected from my purpose and made me realize the vulnerability of my progress.

The cost of incarceration extends beyond what people can imagine. The quiet battles fought in the mind, strain the spirit and fracture family bonds. Yet, for those who make it through, it's a testament to their ability to rise above what was meant to break them.

The wounds of incarceration also influences the nation's economy. The Brennan Center for Justice reported that formerly incarcerated individuals experience a 50 percent reduction in annual earnings, losing nearly half a million dollars in potential income over their lifetimes. This loss does not just affect them, it ripples through entire communities as local, state, and federal governments forfeit tax revenue and the benefits of productive labor.

When returning citizens are properly prepared for reentry, they can contribute meaningfully to the workforce, support their families, and help stabilize the very economies once strained by their absence.

Important Facts:

- Annual cost of incarceration per inmate: $36,000 to $46,000 (Washington University in St. Louis). www.wustl.edu

- Lost earnings due to incarceration and criminal records: $372 billion annually (Brennan Center for Justice). www.brennancenter.org

- Family financial burden: 63% of families with incarcerated loved ones bear court-related costs, with women accounting for 83% (National Institute of Corrections). www.nicic.gov

- Prison wages: Between $0.23 and $1.35 per hour for UNICOR jobs (Federal Bureau of Prisons).

www.unicor.gov

- Commissary expenses for families: Thousands of dollars for phone calls, visits, and basic needs (Prison Policy Initiative).

  www.prisonpolicy.org

RACIAL INJUSTICE

How can you say you love God whom you've never seen
Yet see your brother every day
And can't love him as a human being?

Contrary to popular belief
This is a clear-cut manifestation of outright institutionalized racism
Making a living off another's human suffering that's the agenda

The majority of cheap labor is in warehouses and prison industries
Peep the power we possess working in these factories
Commodities scattered across the nation
Yet, minorities make up 68% of the prison population

There's never been a war on drugs
It's always been a war on Blacks
Not one white person for nearly a decade
Until 1995 was convicted for crack

President Clinton's so-called "poverty tour"

Promised economic growth for the poor

Camouflaged by drug treatment and drug prevention for UNICOR

Minorities became the scapegoats in America's drug war

What goes around comes around...

Now it's knocking at their door

Whites account for 64% of all people using crack

But they paint the picture with our skin...

How real is that?

Who can protect us from harm?

Planes crashing... buildings falling... without an alarm

Evil tyrants turning evil days into opportunity

Killing innocent people within our community

Our souls are thirsting for God

To build the human family instead of graveyards

CHAPTER 4

Dignity and Respect:
A System in Question

Society assumes that prisoners are treated with dignity and respect because the prison system claims to have regulations, rights, and oversight. But this couldn't be further from the truth. Life behind bars strips away the very core of what it means to be human. In prison, you are not just deprived of freedom, you are deprived of your humanity.

For 14 years, I saw firsthand how the system breaks people down, not just physically but mentally, emotionally, and spiritually. The system is not built to care; it is built to profit from every broken piece.

That truth becomes painfully clear when it comes to medical needs. I was battling a severe headache behind my right eye. My vision blurred, the pain was unbearable, and the bright lights stabbed like knives. During the night, every hour dragged, the throbbing refusing to let me rest. I endured it until morning, while waiting for Sick Call, a system similar to an emergency clinic but only available in the early hours.

When I saw the prison doctor, his response was as numbing as the pain itself. He diagnosed me with Bell's palsy, explaining it could result from stress or an infection. Instead of a real treatment plan, he handed me a bottle of Motrin and said it would resolve on its own. Outside of prison, Bell's palsy is treated with steroids, antivirals, and therapy to prevent lasting damage. Inside, I was sent back to my cell with painkillers and empty reassurances.

The next morning, I woke up with an unshakable numbness. As I swung my legs out of bed and shuffled to the mirror, reality hit me hard. The right side of my face had fallen, as if gravity had claimed it overnight. Panic crept in as I stared, frozen, trying to understand what was happening. It wasn't just how it looked, but how it felt: strange, detached, unresponsive.

At that moment, my reflection was more than a medical diagnosis. It was proof that the prison system's indifference was not just an idea. It was carved into me, personal and undeniable.

The next month was miserable. I could only eat on one side of my mouth, and food slipped from the corner, leaving me drooling uncontrollably. My right eye would not close properly, and any light, whether from the sun or a fluorescent bulb, felt like an attack. I bought sunglasses to cope.

Still, even that turned against me. Wearing sunglasses indoors raised suspicion among officers. They questioned me repeatedly: "Why are you wearing those? Are you high? Are you taking something?" No matter how many times I explained my condition, they did not believe me.

I was forced to take urine tests, urinating under supervision to prove I was not using drugs. The humiliation was relentless, and every attempt to help myself made me more of a target. In prison, managing a health crisis can make you a suspect.

Fortunately, my condition eventually improved. For others, untreated medical issues led to permanent scars. I can recall, one afternoon during a game of softball a guy from North Carolina slid into home plate. The base, which should have been properly secured to the ground, shifted as he slid. Normally, bases are anchored firmly to prevent movement.

His foot got caught under the base, causing his ankle to twist violently. The sight was unforgettable, his foot barely connected dangled like a broken limb from a tree. His injury clearly required emergency surgery, but instead of rushing him to get medical care, the guard handcuffed and escorted him to the Special Housing Unit (SHU) to keep him safe. However, he sat in solitary confinement for two weeks before being taken to the hospital. Yet another layer of the harsh brutality of prison.

He was never the same. He walked with a limp, a constant reminder of an injury that could have been properly treated, if those running the prison cared enough to act. This is the result of a system that reduces care to Motrin and indifference.

The SHU was designed to keep things safe and orderly. Looking back, it was another tool that was used to rob us of our dignity, deepen scars, and a reminder that we were never meant to heal.

Imagine being locked down in a room that measures roughly 6 by 9 feet, or about the size of a parking space or elevator for 23 hours a day. I was only sent there a few times and was stripped of even the smallest comforts like warm meals, soft bedding, and the ability to move freely. Food arrived without flavor, and the shower water felt like needles piercing my skin. To cope, I saved butter packets from breakfast to use as lotion after my weekly showers. It may sound absurd, but that butter was a small way of clinging to my pride.

Days were filled with relentless noise from officers doing counts, staff walking through, and the clamor of meal trays being delivered. At night, the noise settled, and that's when we'd engage in what we called "fishing." Using a piece of string tied to something small like a toothpaste tube or pencil, we'd send lines sliding under cell doors to hook onto another inmate's line. It was how we shared books, letters, or magazines, expressing a small act of defiance and connection. These moments of ingenuity and resistance revealed that even in the darkest places, there's still room to find meaning.

I often thought about the movie *Life*. In one scene, Ray Gibson imagined the "boom boom room" as his dream club and escape from the harsh reality of prison. The SHU forced me to create my own version of that. I imagined being free, laughing with my kids, and feeling the sun on my face. Those dreams became my lifeline, helping me hold on to the belief that one day, I would be free.

As of 2023, Black Americans made up about 37% of the state and federal prison population, despite representing only 13.7% of the U.S. population. In contrast, white Americans, who make up about 58.4% of adults, account for just 31% of prisoners.

These disparities are further highlighted by incarceration rates per 100,000 individuals: Black Americans are imprisoned at a rate of about 901 per 100,000, compared to 334 per 100,000 for Hispanic Americans, and 165 per 100,000 for white Americans. This means Black Americans are incarcerated at approximately five times the rate of white Americans. These numbers are not just statistics; they reflect a lived reality and a deeply inequitable system.

My story is not unique. Thousands of men and women are enduring these same conditions, waiting for someone to recognize their value. Among the many challenges we face, even something as basic as sleep becomes a daily struggle. Prisons are too cold in the winter or unbearably hot in the summer.

The lights never go off in some facilities, and guards bang doors and shine flashlights into cells every hour throughout the night to ensure no one has escaped. Emergency counts at 3 or 4 a.m. jolt you awake, and the noise of the unit is constant. For many, the unit's final standing count happens just before midnight, while those working the first kitchen shift are up by 3 a.m. Breakfast is served at 6 a.m., but if you need to visit sick call or wait in the pill line, you could miss it entirely.

The lack of sleep isn't just exhausting, it's damaging. Sleep deprivation affects every part of the body, and when combined with poor nutrition and limited medical care, it becomes a recipe for chronic illness. Incarcerated people are at higher risk for diabetes, high blood pressure, and even HIV. The Eighth Amendment of the U.S. Constitution prohibits "cruel and unusual" punishment, including denying prisoners access to necessary health care, but reality does not reflect that right.

The neglect didn't stop at a lack of care; it shaped the environment we were forced to survive in. One morning, I woke up and stepped into a nightmare: the sewer backed up, covering the bathroom floor in urine and feces. The stench was overwhelming, making it nearly impossible to breathe without gagging. Yet there was no choice. No matter how carefully you tried to step over the filth, there was no avoiding it to reach the shower or the sink. Imagine brushing your teeth while the smell of feces and urine hung heavy in the air. Each breath carried the contamination closer, making the simple act of cleaning yourself feel pointless.

The feces and urine was not cleaned up until later that evening, forcing us to face that unsanitary insult all day. The bacteria, the exposure, and the psychological toll did not matter to those in authority. That is the kind of inhumane treatment that strips away dignity and leaves you questioning if anyone even sees you as human.

The damage of incarceration is not only physical or financial—it runs deeper. The emotional toll is just as heavy. Many people in prison go through phases that parallel the five stages of grief: denial, anger, bargaining, depression, and acceptance, a framework made famous by Elisabeth Kübler-Ross. Prolonged imprisonment weakens executive functioning skills like attention, memory, problem-solving, and emotional regulation. Even now, I struggle to remember the faces and names of people I grew up with. That is an everlasting scar left by a system built to dehumanize.

Prison is a punishment, yes, but it should not come at the cost of basic humanity. People behind bars are still people. They deserve food, rest, and care, not just because the law says so, but because it is the right thing to do.

Prison should not just hold people accountable, but give them the chance to come out better than they went in. If we want to reduce recidivism, we need to focus on rebuilding lives.

Important Facts:

- The Bureau of Prisons lists that 38.3% of federal inmates are Black.

  Federal Bureau of Prisons—Inmate Race Statistics

- The U.S. Sentencing Commission (USSC) reports that 34.9% of individuals in federal prison are Black.

  U.S. Sentencing Commission—Individuals in Federal Bureau of Prisons: Quick Facts

- The Bureau of Justice Statistics (BJS) shows that about 32% of sentenced prisoners nationwide (state and federal combined) are Black, as of year-end 2022.

  BJS—Prisoners in 2022 Report (PDF)

In 2023, Black Americans made up about 37% of the U.S. prison and jail population, nearly three times their share of the overall U.S. population (around 13%).

prisonpolicy.org

- The staff-to-inmate ratio in many federal prisons is often one guard to 300 inmates (Federal Bureau of Prisons).

www.bop.gov

- Policy Statement 541.12 says inmates are to be treated respectfully, impartially, and fairly by staff, without discrimination based on race, religion, sex, disability, or political beliefs. But this is often not the reality (Federal Bureau of Prisons).

www.bop.gov

- The SHU is used as a punishment to silence inmates who speak out, not just for behavior but for requesting basic respect (Sentencing Project).

www.sentencingproject.org

- The influx of reentry programs is a step forward, but they must be built on a foundation of real respect and care, not just as a "check the box" (Prison Policy Initiative).

www.prisonpolicy.org

LOST WITHIN

I thought of a plan to escape bondage

Beyond the boundaries of this physical being I can't fully comprehend

To establish a relationship with Dr. King, Tupac, and Malcolm X…

I want it all, prison was just my slow death

Kept from the heavens through circumstances, I chase misleading views

Abandoned God's word only to turn away from good judgment

In some processes it helps to avoid the pressure that constantly brews

Driven by inhuman and undivine developments, I continue to pursue

These realities will remain as long as I find excuses

The anger spills over into rage

Altering my subconscious state of mind

Leaving me with dark blue dreary days

Fooling myself into thinking I'm going through a sad phase

Giving up on myself

Donating my life to these worldly affairs

That don't love me and can't love me back

Searching for peace in pain that only keeps me off track

Still praying for change

Contributing my soul to the hellfire is just as useless

Life shrinks and expands in proportion

These mind-boggling dimensions

They're only an antidote, taking away my focus

Like a penny with a hole in it I'm hopeless

No focus

Drug dealing was my hocus pocus

No joke, this was my way of thinking

In the club drinking

Females winking and blinking...

Damn, what a life I chose

But more importantly, what a mind I froze

Now, it's a topic I must unfold

I have to be bold

All the rocks I threw at the prison...

All the drugs I sold

I was a cold... mu'tha'

Shut your mouth

Were the gates put up to keep criminals in...

Or keep Congress out?

CHAPTER 5

Education or Rehabilitation:
Justice or Just-US

When entering prison, I carried the weight of my decisions with me. I was determined to use my time behind bars to reform. With that I had a resolute focus. However, that did not shield me from the harsh realities of incarceration.

In some ways, going into prison felt like a strange relief compared to the chaos of the county jail. The cells were originally designed for two men, but overcrowding turned them into three man cells. Things unraveled even more when men were forced to sleep in the common area, which was the space normally used for watching TV, playing cards, or writing letters. There, we were confined to a pod with no fresh air. Mattresses lined the floor, leaving little room for movement and privacy was completely out of the question.

The rare privilege of going outside meant playing basketball in a small enclosed area, where the only view was the sky. Ten-foot-high brick walls surrounded us, with just a narrow opening at the top. We wore the same jumpsuit for an entire week, along with cheap shoes with thin rubber soles. Meals were bland, processed, and barely enough to sustain us. Commissaries mostly offered junk food, a poor substitute that provided overpriced options.

Visits came once a week, and even then we were separated by thick glass, talking through a telephone. Survival was reduced to its simplest form—limited, restricted, monotonous. Federal prison was more structured. The routines gave the illusion of control, yet what prison delivered was tension and unpredictability at every turn.

Learning the unspoken rules, navigating the environment, and preparing for the long road ahead was critical.

After leaving the county jail, I was shipped to Metropolitan Detention Center in Brooklyn, where I stayed for 65 days before being transferred again. From Brooklyn, buses took us to a private airport for the next leg of the journey. As the buses pulled up, one after another, inmates were unloaded into the freezing December rain.

The thin coats and jumpsuits they gave us provided little protection against the biting cold. Handcuffs and shackles bound us tightly, the cold steel pressing into our skin, turning icy from the rain that soaked through everything.

Each drop seemed to amplify the chill, and the weight of the chains felt heavier with every passing minute. For about 20 minutes, we endured that cold, damp misery, a stark reminder of how little humanity we were afforded.

When we finally reached the plane, I couldn't help but stare. The plane looked worn and patched together, with what looked like duct tape visibly covering parts of the wing. It reminded me of *Con Air*, the 1997 movie starring Nicolas Cage about transporting dangerous criminals. Despite my fears I boarded, and we flew to Oklahoma City.

That first day in Oklahoma, I spent hours wrapped in a blanket, clutching cups of hot chocolate and coffee as often as I could get them, trying to thaw out. Although I left the freezing rain behind, the chill lingered. The cold from standing in the December rain settled deep in my body, and it felt like no amount of heat could shake it.

We stayed in Oklahoma for 35 days before boarding another plane that took us to a private airport. From there, buses carried us to Terre Haute Prison in Indiana, where inmates were sent from different institutions across the country. I stayed there for 45 days before being transferred again.

Finally, I arrived in Cumberland, Maryland, where I knew the majority of my sentence would be spent.. With that being said, I thought things would improve. But as the years went on, I realized I was wrong. Every day felt like a repeat of the last: the same clothes, the same food, the same walls, and the same faces. Quickly, I came to understand that the prison system was not designed to educate or rehabilitate any of us. It was a holding place, a system meant to keep inmates stagnant, rather than help us prepare for life after release.

Prison was not going to give me the tools to succeed in the outside world. If I wanted to leave with any sense of purpose, I had to create my own path.

I worked diligently and poured myself into writing 8 books and more than 300 poems. Every word I wrote was a fight against the conditions around me, and I bled for it, literally.

Night after night, in the stillness of my cubicle pressing the pencil against the page started to become unbearable. My skin swelled, blistered, and eventually broke open. Blood and pus oozed out, but I didn't stop. I shifted my grip, writing with my index finger and thumb. To keep it from getting worse, I used some stamps to buy tape, cotton balls, and disinfectant wipes from a guy in the prison hospital. When that was no longer an option, I wrapped my fingers with a torn sock, strips of cloth, or toilet paper.

One evening, I decided to write in the day room instead of my cubicle to get a change of scenery. Sitting at a small table, completely engulfed in my writing, I noticed the man at the microwave. He stood there for what felt like an unusually long time to be warming up soup. Finally, I realized something was not right. Looking around the empty TV room, my gut feeling told me to get out of there.

I gathered my things and rushed out. Just before I made it to my cubicle, I heard the most agonizing scream. When I turned to look in that direction, I froze, staring in shock and disbelief. What I saw could have been a scene in a horror movie. With every touch and every scream, he peeled a layer of skin from his face. His arms were blistered, his face raw, and his screams piercing my soul. He was deteriorating in front of me.

The next day, I pieced it all together after hearing all the rumors and gossip, better known as "inmate.com." The man at the microwave had been cooking a scalding mixture of baby oil, grits, rice, oatmeal, and raisins, heating it for hours. He then poured it on him in an act of calculated violence over a dispute on the basketball court, and disrespect in the unit.

That night still haunts me to this day. The piercing scream, the sight of his skin, is an example of the trauma some endure in prison, a place where violence and pain are a part of daily life.

Even in such a brutal environment, programs such as Father Within or Anger Management provided moments of relief. Still, the system fell far short of what was truly needed.

Statistics show that 67% of incarcerated fathers don't have a high school diploma or GED. While some earn their GED behind bars, that is often where the education ends. Vocational training programs were only offered to those with 18 months or less left on their sentence, leaving long-term inmates like me without opportunities to learn meaningful skills.

Every year, 600,000 inmates are released from prison, and many of them struggle to find employment. Studies show that 83% of ex-offenders who violate parole are unemployed at the time of their violation. Without vocational training, apprenticeship programs, or real educational opportunities, the system sets inmates up for failure, making it harder for them to succeed after release.

The Bureau of Prisons focuses on keeping inmates distracted. Rehabilitation requires more than just passing time. It requires education, preparation, and support that can empower them to rebuild their lives.

One of the few bright spots I witnessed during my time in prison came with President Obama's administration. The Fair Sentencing Act of 2010 reduced the sentencing disparity between crack cocaine and powder cocaine from 100-to-1 to 18-to-1. This change addressed a major injustice that had disproportionately affected Black and brown inmates.

The law did not just apply to future cases, it was retroactive. I saw men who were sentenced to life under the old law have their sentences commuted to time served. Many of these men were freed after decades, finally reuniting with their families. Men spent years believing they would die in prison. It was a powerful moment, but also a reminder of how broken the system is. Those men should have never been serving such harsh sentences in the first place. In federal prison a life sentence is just that. YOUR OUT DATE SAYS DECEASED.

After my release, I held on to three different jobs to stay afloat. My first was at a homeless shelter in Cleveland during the winter months. My second job was seasonal landscaping work for the City of Cleveland during the summer. My first permanent job came at U.S. Foods. Eventually, when I moved to Columbus, Ohio, I landed a position as a distribution clerk. I held that role for 7.5 years. My dedication paid off and I advanced out of the warehouse to one of the optical stores as an apprentice optician. Altogether, I spent 11.5 years with the company, confronting racism. Despite consistently earning top performance reviews in the warehouse, and quickly becoming the store's leading salesperson, with exceptional customer feedback, I was denied promotions. I fought for pay raises others seemed to receive effortlessly. I advocated for every possible opportunity, including cross-training that would have allowed me to develop new skills and expand into additional roles.

The ruthless work environment carried echoes of prison. Managers would yell at me in front of patients, slamming their hands on tables in outbursts of blatant disrespect. I arrived at work one day to find my lab coat covered in slurs written with a permanent marker, a clear message meant to degrade me. I suited up everyday like a soldier on the battlefield and pushed through layers of bias, humiliation, and bureaucracy to demand equality.

Rebuilding the relationships with my children was another challenge entirely. My son had grown into a young man. When I came home, there was a quiet barrier between us, built on years of missed birthdays, graduations, and other milestones. My daughter, on the other hand, seemed more willing to connect, but even then, rebuilding the bond required patience and understanding.

In prison, I learned to focus solely on myself—my needs, my wants, and my survival. But outside, everything was different. Suddenly, my choices had to include others. I was learning how to be present in their lives to support them emotionally, and bridge the gap created by my absence.

The struggles of reentry tested me in ways I could not have imagined. But each test strengthened my resolve and reminded me of why I fought so hard for my freedom. It is not enough to survive reentry. You must adapt, and create a life that reflects the person you have worked so hard to become.

Now, as a Reentry/Community Resource Coordinator, I have the privilege of helping others navigate their own journeys, offering the support and resources I wish I had when I was released. None of this is happening because the prison system offered me rehabilitation. Looking back, I did that.

My book *Begin, Believe, Become* serves as the foundation for my life skills curriculum focusing on interpersonal growth and transformation. The same process that helped me rebuild my life from the inside out is the catalyst to guide others as they discover their own strength and begin writing a new chapter in their own lives. Each module, from Self-Awareness and Self-Approval to Facing Your Fears and Breaking the Cycle, was birthed through my experiences. These principles guided me through the toughest years of my life, teaching me how to grow, heal, and lead with purpose.

The system did not give me what I needed to succeed, so I created my own opportunities. I stayed up late, pushed through pain, and prepared myself for life after prison. But even then, I was not fully prepared for the challenges of reentry.

Now, I am committed to helping others find their way, offering them the tools and resources to live by my motto: *begin, believe, become* - to be the best versions of themselves.

Important Facts:

- Fair Sentencing Act (2010): Reduced the sentencing disparity from 100-to-1 to 18-to-1 for crack vs. powder cocaine (Sentencing Project).
www.sentencingproject.org

- 67% of incarcerated fathers don't have a high school diploma or GED (Bureau of Justice Statistics).
www.bjs.ojp.gov

- 83% of parole violators are unemployed at the time of their violation (Bureau of Justice Statistics).
www.bjs.ojp.gov

- The Federal Bureau of Prisons focuses on distractions rather than educational reform (Harvard Politics).
www.harvardpolitics.com

- 600,000 inmates are released annually, many without proper reentry support (Bureau of Justice Statistics). www.bjs.ojp.gov

THE CIRCLE OF LIFE AS A MAN

As a man, I tried so hard to hide my feelings

Caught in a sea of emotions

Dealing with bad choices, trauma, and mental illness

It wasn't about the things I did

The road I paved for those who took advantage of my kindness, integrity,

and willingness

As a man, unconditional love felt more like love with conditions

Judged on my worth through finances and billings

Momma said, "Work hard, pay your bills, raise your children

Love your wife no matter how she looks

Because she won't always be appealing"

If I could tell you anything

Momma was right

But she didn't see the darkness, the confusion, the hurtful nights

She didn't see the emotional abuse, the lonely, battered syndrome fights

She didn't see the pain I hid from her

The pain I hid from the world

I tried to hide my pain from myself

Holding onto a pill bottle, a gun, and an urge

I curbed my apologies with these bullets I hugged

Sweeping my feelings under a rug

Reminiscing on the prison floors I scrubbed

Stereotyped as cold-hearted, a menace, and a thug

Who do I run to as a man

When my heart has been bitten by a controlling love bug

Wrapped in a silhouette of a vicious cycle of mean-mugs

As a man, I had no one to run to

No one to talk to who would understand how I felt

I didn't want to be seen as unbothered, selfish, or weak

I'm a college grad with a degree

Still, I couldn't express my unique

So I chose to stay silent, fearing how they'd critique

As a man, this is my reality

I gave my all in forever, but forever isn't a guarantee

I suffered through backstabbing and entitled blasphemy

As a man, I get emotional when I look inside Clutching onto a blunt, a bottle of liquor

Drowning my pain just to survive

Using drugs and women for an emotional high

Killing my dreams like a round of pesticide

As a man, I've been through it all

Selling drugs, destroying my community just to ball

Facing life as a criminal, I told myself I wanted it all

I had everything and lost it all

Bounced back from nothing and stood tall

People turned on me, praying for my downfall

As a man, it's hard to put my thoughts to rest

Chasing a bad feeling I ignored with neglect

Against all odds, to no man do I confess

The circle of life I chase, the circle of time I waste

The circle of love and energy has been my greatest asset

Yet, the circle of choosing me first has been my biggest regret

As a man, the circle of confusion eats at my intention

Questioning what I provided as a man

Second-guessing my own reflection

Relationships are like quicksand

One moment, you're living your best life, the life you planned

The next, you're drowning in a reality you don't understand

This is the circle of life, so hard to comprehend

CHAPTER 6

When Solutions Become Problems:
Reflection or Deflection

It has been said that prison somehow strengthens family bonds, fostering deeper emotional connections despite the separation. I'm almost certain whoever said that has never been to prison. In fact, it dismantles those connections, leaving fractured relationships and emotional scars difficult to heal. Time in prison taught me that far from encouraging family ties, the system erodes them, creating barriers that are hard if not impossible to overcome.

In rare moments, some connections within prison walls offered a sense of humanity. However complicated or fleeting they may have been, we held those times close to our hearts.

One such connection was with a prison guard, whose attention began with harmless compliments but evolved into something more layered and complex. At the time, I had been locked up for over six years and the officers knew me well. Typically officers were only assigned to a unit for a quarter before they rotated to another assignment.

One night during third shift I was up writing under my nightlight, as I often did. The two officers on duty were making their rounds for the 3 a.m. count. As they moved through the unit shining their flashlights on each bunk, they stopped briefly. When the female officer shined her light on me she giggled and said, "Why are you up most nights?" "Writing," I responded. "About?" she asked, the beam of her flashlight dropping down slightly toward my lower body. "Stuff" I replied, trying hard not to get distracted.

For the rest of the night I could not focus. I kept replaying our interaction in my mind, wondering if I had imagined her tone and expression. I did not expect to see her much after that since she already completed her one quarter in the unit. However, the following week I was surprised to see her reassigned to my unit, this time on the first shift.

From there, our interactions became more frequent. The flirting continued, subtle but unmistakable: smiles, glances, and lingering stares that seemed to hold unspoken conversations. As one of the janitors in the unit, I often went to her office to empty the trash or mop the floor. This gave us brief opportunities to talk, and with each exchange, tension between us grew stronger.

On her last day of work for the quarter, that tension finally came to a head. I asked to clean her office, a routine task that involved tidying up the space. Before getting started, I realized some supplies were needed and asked her to unlock the supply room.

Normally an officer would either hold the door open or stand outside while I grabbed what was required, but this time was different. I intentionally timed my request when chicken was being served on the compound, that was the one time everyone showed up at the chow hall. So I knew the unit would be nearly empty.

She followed me into the supply room, closing the door behind her. What happened next left me stunned. It had been six years since I had sex. It felt surreal, I did not want it to end. That moment stayed with me until I saw her working in the visitation room.

One of the women who visited me regularly became a target of harassment fueled by jealousy from the officer. She was forced to endure that added tension, on top of the usual challenges that come with visiting someone in prison.

The officer's interference did not stop when she transferred. She was always lurking in the background, keeping me on edge. On multiple occasions, the officer falsely claimed her clothes violated the dress code. Her name would mysteriously be missing from the visitor's list, forcing her to wait while they "searched" for her information. These tactics were intended to frustrate and discourage her from continuing to visit. Even when the officer left my unit to work in the visitation room, she continued to find ways to disrupt my life.

One day, I was surprised to see her back in the unit. She must have been assigned to special duty or covering another officer's shift. Her presence caught me off guard.

I was mopping my area when she called me to her office to empty the trash. When I walked in and saw her sitting at the desk, I could feel the tension instantly. As I kneeled down to grab the trash from under her desk, my face ended up between her legs. She did not move away. Instead, she grabbed my head and pushed my face closer. "You will never get this again," she said. I stood up, stunned, and turned to leave, but she was not done. "Don't go back to your room," she added. "Why?" I asked. "I'm shaking you down for contraband," she answered. At any time, an officer can shake down your room, looking for contraband. Contraband can be anything an officer deems to be a violation of the institution's rules and regulations.

When I returned, my room was a mess. Clothes from my foot locker were thrown onto my bed, and the items in my wall locker were scattered all over the floor.

Frustrated, I walked back to her office, closed the door, and confronted her. It felt like we were at home, in a relationship, arguing about me cheating on her or a disagreement over finances. She was in my face, and I was in hers, until our lips touched. Pushing me away, she said, "You need to leave before I write you up for disobeying a direct order."

I left her office with the taste of her lips and the scent of her perfume lingering. That day, she worked a double shift, and just before the 3 a.m. count, we found ourselves in the supply room, tearing each other's clothes off once again.

The following weekend another woman friend, who had been visiting me for over two years, enduring the long 6 hour drive from Detroit, was inexplicably removed from my visitation list. Despite this she remained consistent and put in the effort to stay connected in person. However, our visits were not without interruptions. The officer always found a reason to come over during our time together. She would make comments about us holding hands, how we were sitting, or that we "violated" the one-kiss-in, one-kiss-out rule. Yet, another jealous attempt to frustrate me.

One particular visit escalated beyond her usual antics. The officer accused us of exchanging contraband, and the lieutenant was called. I was escorted out of the visitation room, taken to the lieutenant's office, strip-searched, and placed in the hole under investigation. My visitor was escorted off the compound, humiliated, and told she would be under further review. That moment changed everything.

When I got out of the hole, I tried everything within my power to rectify the situation. I spoke with my unit manager, wrote letters to the warden, I even reached out to the investigating officer and the lieutenant, pleading with them to review the videotape. I knew the video would prove our innocence. However, my pleas went unheard.

The next time she planned to visit me, I went to the visitation room, eagerly waiting to see her, only to find out she was removed from my list. I called her afterwards, and we tried to make sense of what happened. For months, we exchanged phone calls and letters, clinging to the connection we'd built over the years. Then one day, my calls went unanswered. The letters ceased, and I had nothing but memories.

Prison rules make every visit a battle. There are countless restrictions and hoops to jump through. When family members or friends can make the trip, they are met with policies designed to dehumanize and discourage them. No one can truly connect with their loved one when a simple hug is considered a violation of the rules.

The rules of visitation are not structured to support family ties. Simple gestures like holding hands or embracing a loved one are often met with stern warnings or outright punishment.

During visits, my mother would bring my son and daughter, sometimes accompanied by one or two of my nieces or nephews. Those moments should have been filled with love and connection, but were often interrupted by the staff. My daughter could not sit on my lap, and my son was not allowed to hold my hand. If I kissed them on the cheek, I would be called to the officer's desk and threatened to have my visit cut short. Even when they behaved perfectly, the officers would find reasons to impose restrictions, creating an emotional distance that mirrored the physical separation of incarceration.

One visit stands out vividly in my mind. My mother brought both my son and daughter for a visit. My son, full of energy and excitement, kept tugging at my sleeve. "Daddy, take me to get some popcorn. Daddy, let's go get some candy. Daddy, can we get some chips?" I told him "we would go later, or that I couldn't right now." He cried, not understanding why I continued to make excuses. The truth was, I was not allowed to take him to the vending machines. A yellow line separated inmates from the vending area, we were forbidden to cross it. I didn't have the courage to tell my son that I could not do something as simple as walking with him to get a snack.

After that visit, I felt broken. What made the visit even harder was what followed. Entering and leaving the visitation area required a strip search. Each time, I had to stand in front of the officers, bend over, spread my cheeks and cough. Not only did I feel ashamed that I could not fulfill my son's simple request. I was also humiliated yet again, and reminded of prison's impact on my life.

That day something shifted inside of me. It was my breaking point, my "aha" moment. I promised myself to never again put myself in a position where someone could dictate how I interacted with my children.

For those of us who are incarcerated far from home, visits become rare. Many prisons are located hundreds of miles from their family, making travel both expensive and exhausting. This geographical separation, coupled with stringent visitation policies, makes it extremely difficult to maintain strong family connections.

Letters become your lifeline. "Mail Call" was a ritual, an adventure all its own, every weekday after the 4 p.m. count. Men would line up, waiting for the correction officer to bring the mail, hoping their name would be called. Hearing your name meant someone cared enough to not only think about you but also write to you. However, when your name was not called, it felt like a blow. It magnified the distance, isolation, and emptiness during incarceration.

Those moments of silence could weigh heavily, leading to stress and loneliness that were hard to shake. Still, the anticipation of mail calls kept many of us going.

Phone calls were another constant challenge. We were allotted only 300 minutes per month, broken into 15-minute intervals. Rationing out those minutes between my children, the two women in my life, and my family, was a daunting task. It was not just about managing time, but balancing the weight of those relationships and longing to stay connected.

Like anything else on the compound, people found ways to work around the restrictions. If someone did not use their 300 minutes, you could buy the time he had by adding your numbers to his phone list. This was a hustle that worked for a while but always came at a risk. If the same number appeared on two different lists, it would not take long for the administration to notice. An investigation would follow, leading to write-ups, loss of privileges, or even time in the hole.

Over time, the weight of maintaining these connections began to take its toll. The distance, the rules, and the constant challenges chipped away at the bonds I worked so hard to maintain. As the months turned into years, some of my loved ones simply could not bear the strain any longer. One by one, they drifted away, leaving behind the hollow ache of separation that prison enforces so well.

Yet, in the void left by those losses, something unexpected emerged, a bond with other men stripped of everything. In prison, without cars, jewelry, or distractions, you are left with nothing but the essence of who you are. I met men from my hometown of Cleveland, Washington, D.C., Detroit, Baltimore, Buffalo, and beyond. I also met people from around the world, including Puerto Rico, Venezuela, The Dominican Republic, and Africa. Men I would never have known if life had unfolded differently. Together, we formed something real. We did not have much, but we had each other.

Our connection was not built on appearances or material things. It was built during the silence of long nights, through shared struggle, and over stories with no pretense. We would walk the narrow hallways of dormitories sectioned off by cubicles, walk the track for hours talking, or just sit in the unit exchanging stories of who we were before incarceration, describing our cities and neighborhoods. I could look across the yard and know that these men had my back, just as I had theirs.

The bonds I made inside prison were different. Reduced to nothing, we found a brotherhood that outlasted the gates, the time, and the distance. And that is something prison could not take from us.

Even now, years after our release, those bonds remain unbroken. Out of nowhere, I'll get a call from one of my partners in Baltimore and another from D.C. One of us would add a friend from Buffalo or Kalamazoo to the call and before you know it we would be on the phone for hours. Catching each other up and laughing about funny moments we shared while doing time together. What started behind bars has continued into life after incarceration, revealing even in the darkest places that something good can grow.

Prison is not designed to foster human connections. It is a system that prioritizes control over compassion, and that takes its toll, not just on inmates, but also on the ones we love the most.

Yes, I contributed to the breakdown of my relationships through my actions. However, the system exacerbated it and created barriers that I am still working to overcome.

The withdrawal of some women in my life was a direct result of both my poor decisions and a system designed to erode relationships. These women were my strongest supporters. However, prison policies, the distance, which is purposeful and personal dynamics worked in tandem to sever those bonds.

Family and friends are supposed to be the foundation of support for anyone trying to rebuild their life during incarceration. In prison those ties are treated as an afterthought, if not a burden.

Important Facts:

- Visitation rules often create stress and deter family members from visiting inmates. Long waits, invasive searches, and arbitrary enforcement of dress codes make visits unpleasant and emotionally draining (Prison Policy Initiative).

  www.prisonpolicy.org

- Many prisoners are incarcerated far from their families, making visits difficult and costly. A large percentage of inmates are housed more than 100 miles from home (Prison Policy Initiative).

  www.prisonpolicy.org

- Maintaining family ties can reduce recidivism, but prison policies make it difficult to sustain these connections (Office of Justice Programs).

  www.ojp.gov

NO ONE CAME

No one came when my back was against the wall
Giving me a reason to keep believing, to ease my fall

No one came when it started getting rough
Donating a helpful word or two, someone I could trust

No one came to free me of danger
Leaving me amongst scandalous no-good strangers
Down on my knees, slowly breaking
Knowing I'll be taken away

No one came to provide a little love
A push, a shove
A friendly smile... a warm, everlasting bug
Knowing I hate the damn judge

No one came when I needed support

A familiar face while in court

Praying I don't come up short

Blew trial, whose number can I dial?...

No one came

No one came

Disappointment filled my brain

Don't trip in too deep to place blame

Never would I change

No one came

That's a damn shame

No one came

Never will I place blame

Your main man...

No one came

CHAPTER 7

Sexuality in Prison:
A Double-Edged Sword

Life behind bars comes with challenges that test your assumptions, boundaries, and ways of coping. In this chapter, I confront one of the hardest truths about prison life: how men deal with intimacy, identity, and the choices they make to survive.

Early in my incarceration I was sent to a processing facility. At this facility, some men, known as cadres, worked and lived there full-time while the rest of us were processed through. Cadres handled tasks like distributing laundry, preparing food, and assisting with operations. Their movement around the unit was more unrestricted compared to the rest of us.

One day while on lockdown, I was looking out of the window, which was about the size of a standard envelope, when I witnessed something that shocked me to my core—two men kissing.

I stood frozen, confusion swirling in my mind. I had never seen two men kiss, and the image left me grappling with questions about identity and connection. It wasn't about judgment; it was about facing the reality that people express their identities in ways that might challenge my preconceived notions. For them, that kiss reflected who they were, unaffected by the bars that surrounded us.

For many, this does not necessarily reflect their identity outside of prison, but instead reveals how the environment amplifies unmet needs. Studies highlight the complexity of these dynamics, showing that while 6.2% of men report same-sex encounters at some point in their lives, only a fraction identify as gay or bisexual. This disparity reflects how behavior and identity don't always align, especially in extreme environments like prison.

As the months went by, coping with the lack of human connection became an ongoing struggle. I resorted to masturbation and sometimes managed to watch smuggled porn videos through DVD players. But it was never truly satisfying. It was like putting a Band-Aid over a wound that required stitches.

Each time, I was left feeling more frustrated and emotionally drained. The longing I felt wasn't just physical; it was also deeply emotional. I missed the intimacy of being with a woman, touching, hugging, and feeling a romantic bond. It became a constant reminder of what was missing in my life and how much this deprivation impacted my mental state.

Prisoners cope with the lack of sexual intimacy in different ways. Some rely on fantasy and masturbation, while others develop emotional or physical relationships with fellow inmates. If you were lucky or had money you could pay for sex from a guard or nurse.

After leaving the processing facility, I was transferred to another prison, where I had an experience that further opened my eyes. On the compound, there was a man who worked in the kitchen. He noticed my diet of strictly fruits and vegetables with no beef or pork, and began bringing me apples and oranges. In the beginning, I felt a quiet gratitude for his kindness, but that quickly turned into uneasiness.

It wasn't until I shared this with a friend from my neighborhood, out on the yard, that I learned the truth. My friend explained, "Oh yeah, man, he's trying to get with you. That's what people do in here, they give you things when they want something from you." It was my first time doing time, and I hadn't yet learned the subtle ways men in prison might initiate a relationship. In his case, the fruit was not just an act of kindness; it came with an ulterior motive. The next time, I refused and told him he didn't need to bring anything else. I wanted to make it clear that I was not interested. However, that did not stop his advances. Though he never offered me fruit again, he often stared at me from across the yard, as if his glance would change my mind.

Shift changes brought another layer to the compound's dynamics. Correctional officers and staff had to walk through the yard to report for duty. Despite the risk of being written up or sent to the hole for "reckless eyeballing," men could not help but stare at the two women passing by. One day, just before a shift change, I was on the yard and noticed someone who appeared to be wearing a halter top, lipstick, and had what looked like breasts. At first, I thought it was a woman and wondered how they allowed someone like that on the compound. As I got closer, I realized he was not a woman. One had actual breasts from taking hormone pills, and the other stuffed his shirt with toilet paper to mimic them. They used Kool-Aid for lipstick and sewed their shirts into halter tops. I was blown away. It was shocking, but it also showed me how far people would go to express themselves in an environment designed to suppress individuality.

Another eye-opening experience came from a man in my unit who took me under his wing. Older men in prison often guide younger ones, helping them navigate the system. He gave me a book, *How to Eat to Live* and encouraged me to write down my thoughts in a journal. He knew I wrote poetry, and pushed me to build strategies for my future. In prison, we called these conversations "building." We would talk about plans, write them down, and visualize a better life once released from prison. For the first time, I felt like I had a blueprint for something better.

However, when a new gay inmate moved into our unit, things shifted. The man who mentored me suddenly became distant, always finding excuses not to meet with me. I later learned they knew each other from the outside and were in a relationship. They ended up as bunkmates. I was not upset because he was gay. It was the fact that he lived a life that was the opposite of how he presented himself to me. I respected him for what he taught me, but I could not shake the feeling of betrayal. It wasn't his sexuality that hurt, it was the lack of transparency from someone I had come to trust and admire.

These experiences gave me a clearer understanding of the dynamics in prison. They challenged me to think deeply about human connection and the assumptions I carried.

Learning to navigate these nuances became an essential part of my journey behind bars.

Let me be clear, sexual orientation is deeply rooted and does not simply shift because of environment or isolation. While debates continue about whether it is shaped by genetics, environment, or both, one truth remains: suggesting that it changes due to incarceration distorts the reality of life behind bars and dehumanizes LGBTQ+ individuals. It diminishes their identities while undermining the dignity and authenticity of everyone incarcerated.

Important Facts:

- LGBTQ+ inmates face disproportionately high rates of sexual victimization in prisons and jails (Prison Policy Initiative).

  www.prisonpolicy.org

- Sexual assault remains a significant issue, with many cases going unreported due to fear of retaliation (Bureau of Justice Statistics).

  www.bjs.ojp.gov

WHAT'S LOVE?

Time away from you feels like an eternity
Can't gather my thoughts when you're not next to me

How do I turn back the hands of time?
When the hands of time don't turn back
How do I tell someone I love them?
When love is a fantasy I don't attract?

How do I say goodbye in the still of darkness?
In the still of night?
Trapped in a whirlwind of emotions
No longer staring at the light

Sun-rays of the good days
Wash out in the wake of a hurricane
Some days, I crave the love I gave to you
The love of gravity pulled me to you

It's the love of being loved

It's the love of being loved I want to feel

It's the love of two rivers flowing downhill

I know what love feels like

I've been in love before

I know what love feels like

But love doesn't live here anymore

I was once told:

"I love you unconditionally

I love you to the end of time

I love you to the moon and back

I love you like I never loved before"

Please tell me

Why didn't love love me after I walked through that damn prison door?

Love didn't love me

Love didn't love me

Love is what sets me free

Love is an action verb

Love requires sweat equity

There is no such thing as passive love

There is no such thing as love at first sight

You either love or don't love

You either love or don't love

Love is putting up a fight

Love is a river of water finding its way downhill

It drifts through the valleys, yet never stands still

Love is patience

Love is watching love grow into greatness

Love is an unspoken word

Love is free as a bird

Love doesn't love

Love doesn't love me

Love is what sets me free

Caught in a sea of emotion

Streaming down a lonely river in constant motion

Love is the force that we cannot control

The deepest of feelings, yet it leaves us whole

What's love, if not the reason we fight?

A gentle power, pulling us through the night

What's love?

CHAPTER 8

Don't Drop the Soap:
Beyond the Joke

For every generation, there seems to be a public service announcement (PSA) aimed at instilling fear, anxiety, or at least causing people to think twice before making poor decisions. Whether on television, radio, billboards, or the internet, these slogans have been used to warn individuals, especially teenagers, from repeating past mistakes.

I remember the explosion of crack cocaine bringing us the slogan "Just Say No," and when Magic Johnson announced he was HIV-positive, "Wrap It Up" became a rallying cry. There were always reminders out there, encouraging people to think twice before making dangerous choices. AIDS was the leading cause of death for Black Americans aged 25 to 44 in the late 1990s, and the statistics on sexually transmitted diseases were especially alarming for young Black women. Slogans were everywhere, but in earlier generations, survival didn't come with a catchphrase. We just knew instinctively that to stay alive meant protecting ourselves and family, especially those of us who were Black and fighting for civil rights.

I grew up in an era filled with slogans that aimed to motivate and shape our decisions. One of the most infamous phrases I heard growing up, particularly when it came to prison, was "Don't drop the soap." It was an inside joke, repeated by my older brothers and the men in the neighborhood. They'd say it, laugh, and move on, leaving me curious but uneasy. I never questioned their manhood or doubted who they were, but that phrase stuck with me in a way I didn't fully understand at the time. I didn't grow up in a world where homosexual activity was openly discussed, so the joke just seemed bizarre to me.

It wasn't until I was sent to The Ohio State Reformatory in Mansfield, Ohio, at eighteen that I started to understand the weight of that joke. I was young, small, and scared, thrust into an environment I barely knew how to handle. The first time "Don't drop the soap" really made sense to me was in the prison shower room, infamously called "the car wash." There I was, standing with over 50 men, all showering in the same space, with a long sprinkler-like pipe above us trickling water down. The space was tight, and any wrong move could lead to a dangerous situation, or at least that's how it felt.

In that moment, the phrase became more than just a joke. I realized it was a cautionary tale about maintaining your dignity and avoiding trouble. Constantly aware of my surroundings, I scrubbed my skin with bare hands, no rag, trying to finish quickly and keep my eyes forward. The steam thickened, voices around me blurred, and my pulse hammered in my ears. Every movement felt risky, like one wrong step could set off something I would not be able to control.

I kept telling myself to move fast and stay invisible, but inside I felt exposed, like no matter what I did, danger was waiting. Every motion felt watched, every sound sharper than it should have been. I just wanted to wash fast and get out. I moved the soap carefully over my body, raising my left arm to wash under my arms.

And then it happened.

I dropped the soap.

The hollow smack as it hit the wet floor echoed louder than it should have. My chest tightened, and it felt like every pair of eyes was suddenly on me. Panic set in. I knew I had to pick it up, but fear froze me. I couldn't afford another bar, and asking someone else was unthinkable, breaking the cardinal rule of prison. In that instant, I understood how quickly vulnerability could turn into danger.

That was the moment I truly grasped the meaning behind "Don't drop the soap." It wasn't just a joke about being gay or sexual activity in prison. It was about survival, about protecting yourself and avoiding situations that could leave you exposed to power, control, and exploitation.

Homosexual tendencies don't develop because of prison; they are a part of who someone is long before they arrive. Dropping the soap, in this context, had nothing to do with sexual orientation. It was about the reality of power dynamics and the risks of being caught off guard.

If you drop the soap, leave it. Get another one. No bar is worth your safety. In prison, even something that small can decide whether you stay safe or become a target. Survival is not about strength alone, However, it is about knowing when to step away.

Important Facts:

- The phrase "Don't drop the soap" has been popularized as a euphemism for the fear of sexual assault in prison, trivializing the real trauma experienced by victims (Just Detention International).

  www.justdetention.org

- Media portrayals often reinforce harmful stereotypes about prison sexual violence, normalizing it and distracting from the complex power dynamics present in prisons (International Journal of Criminology and Sociological Theory).

  www.ijcst.com

STILL STANDING

They say change is gonna come
That's why I'm standing here
Standing on the backs of my ancestors' blood, sweat, and tears
We Think to Make Live with our youth to be great
The fruit of revenge is eaten from a cold plate
Top down, bottom up, middle out "Guns down"
Reentry is a marathon

False hopes, broken dreams, empty promises, nothing new
But I'm still standing here, pushing through

I've been connecting the dots
Refuse to associate with the opps
I chose love when my heart did not
No longer cooking drugs with a Pyrex and a pot
I learned the dos and the nots

The rules of the game, thou shalt not plot

I would rather be hated for who I truly am
Than adored for someone I'm truly not
Life is full of fake people who pretend to care about a lot
Giving what they never got
Taking shots... a crab in the basket for my spot

Reality is perception
I've been lied to
Lost so many people in my life felt like I died too

You are the master of your body
The king of your mind
The ruler of your soul
What are you willing to do with what you have
Before you become bitter, tired, and old?

CHAPTER 9

The Realities of Prison Life:
The Role We Play

It was late in the afternoon, and while walking down the hallway lined with cubicles, I saw the situation unfold. A man collapsed, barely breathing, right there between the cubicles. When I reached him, his face was pale, his chest struggling to rise. He overdosed on cocaine. At that moment, the walls of the prison faded into the background. There were no medical staff rushing in, nor guards stepping up to help, just us. The reality inside prison walls is that when something happens, survival depends on the men around you.

I dropped beside him, my hands shaking as I tried to keep him breathing. "Stay with me, man," I kept saying, over and over again, pressing down on his chest. I tilted his head back and began CPR, hoping for a sign of life. Minutes passed like hours, but then, finally, his chest rose again, slowly, weakly, but he was breathing.

No doubt, this death-threatening episode was caused by drugs. You see, drugs circulate inside prison just like money, brought in by visitors, sometimes staff, or hidden in deliveries. The temptation to escape reality through drugs is strong, but the cost is higher than most realize.

We didn't stop to question where the drugs came from; we just fought to keep him alive. That is what it's like in prison. Inmates are not just fighting to survive the violence, but also hidden dangers like drugs, mental distress, and the weight of each day while inside.

Survival in prison is more than physical fights. It is a daily battle for your mental and emotional stability. At the Federal Correctional Institution in Elkton, Ohio, I learned this lesson in another way right on the basketball court. The gym was always packed, not with men waiting to play, but with men watching. The court was the stage where reputations were built.

One day, a hard foul turned into something much bigger. The guy, a Muslim from Philly, called me a word you do not use generally referring to a man but especially not in prison—"a bitch." The moment he said it, everyone in the gym froze, rather than erupting like you'd expect. Instead, a quiet murmur spread through the crowd, the kind of low buzz that carries more weight than noise.

My teammates immediately stepped in, forming a wall between us, while his teammates did the same, trying to contain the tension before it exploded. Our words cut through the air, sharp and full of venom. I was ready for whatever, and I made sure he knew it. I was yelling, trying to push through while they held me back, but deep down I started to realize that no one was going to let this go any further, not yet at least. Reluctantly, I pulled myself together, stayed in the game, and bided my time.

We headed back up the court, and I tried to focus on the game. The ball was passed to me at half court. I made a move to the basket, but nothing was there, so I passed the ball and moved across the lane. That's when I saw him standing there, right in the middle. The opportunity was perfect, and I didn't hesitate. Bam! I hit him.

Before he could throw a punch, my friend from Washington, D.C., jumped in, and the two of us had him on the ground. People scattered from the court and the stands, but no one else threw a punch. It was just the three of us.

The fight was broken up quickly, but confusion filled the gym. People didn't know which side to take or what to do. I was from Ohio, my friend was from Washington, D.C., and the guy we jumped was from Philly and a Muslim. Some men were from Ohio but also part of the Muslim community, while others were from D.C. or Philly and had ties to the same religious group. The gym was full of overlapping loyalties, states, faiths, and friendships, all colliding, leaving everyone uncertain about where to stand.

The next day, there was a call among the different communities and states to settle the issue. Leaders from various groups came together to address what happened, and the beef was resolved before it could escalate further.

It was a stark example of how quickly a single word can spiral into something far bigger, pulling in people who had no part in the original conflict.

In prison, your affiliations matter more than anything else. It didn't matter that I was from Ohio. What mattered were the alliances I built. Men from Washington, D.C., Detroit, Philly, or Baltimore would stand behind you if your ties were strong.

The violence was not only confined to the basketball court. I've seen stabbings over small disputes, where a word or a look could be enough to provoke physical attacks. In prison, everything is a trigger, and it happens so fast that most of the time, the system simply cannot keep up.

While violence is visible, the drug trade is one of the hidden threats in prison. Drugs, cellphones, cigarettes, and "black-and-milds" most commonly make their way inside through staff members. It is not uncommon to see officers escorted off the compound in handcuffs for smuggling in contraband. Several times, I witnessed officers who gave in to the temptation of easy money, risking their careers and freedom for the promise of a quick payoff.

While shipments brought in by vendors and visitors contribute, it is the staff who have the access and opportunity to move items past security. Once the contraband is inside, it's distributed on the yard and fuels a hidden economy that thrives behind the scenes. It is not forced on anyone, but the allure is undeniable. And once someone gets hooked, whether on drugs, alcohol, or gambling, the cycle begins.

Families often have no idea that the money they send is not being used for commissary or phone calls. Instead, it's funneled into feeding addictions or paying debts, perpetuating a system that staff members help sustain. The impact of this cycle stretches far beyond prison walls, touching everyone connected to it.

Once drugs are in circulation, the price skyrockets. A bag of marijuana, which would cost $100 on the street, could go for thousands inside. An amount as small as the cap of a ChapStick tube could cost $50. And while not everyone gets involved, for those who do, it's a dangerous game that can lead to serious financial, physical, and mental consequences. Inmates hooked on drugs often lie to their families, asking for money under false pretenses. They falsely claim the money is needed for supplies, when truthfully, it enables them to feed their addiction. The pressure grows, and with it comes the risk of extortion. Once they get in too deep, the consequences can be severe.

Not only can physical violence leave scars, but the mental toll in prison is just as devastating. I remember a man from New York, who after five years inside, completely unraveled. He started pacing the yard, talking to himself, disconnected from reality. The pressure broke him. It is a common story that men lose more than their freedom in prison. They lose themselves. The constant need to be on guard, daily stress, and the weight of survival, all eats away at you. And the worst part is, many hide their struggles out of fear. Showing weakness in prison can be fatal.

Federal prisons claim to protect inmates from violence, gangs, and mental breakdowns. On paper, the policies look good; the monitoring systems, mental health support, and the use of special housing units (SHUs), often referred to as "the hole." These units are designed to separate inmates who are deemed a threat to others or themselves, or who need protection. The idea is to maintain safety by isolating individuals in single or double cells for 23 hours a day.

The actual outcome of these abusive control methods speak differently than the paper trail. In 2024, suicide deaths in state prisons across the U.S. rose sharply, with several systems reporting numbers that more than doubled compared to the previous year. Meanwhile, in federal prisons that same year, 22 inmates died by suicide, underscoring how widespread the crisis has become. Overall, the suicide rate in U.S. prisons increased from about 0.24 per 1,000 people in 2013 to 0.76 per 1,000 in 2024. This steady rise over the past decade shows a crisis that can no longer be ignored.

These numbers highlight the growing mental health crisis within the prison system, underscoring the lack of adequate support and intervention for those who are most vulnerable.

Overcrowding and understaffing contribute to the daily violence and unchecked mental health crises. On some days, a single officer is responsible for monitoring hundreds of inmates. In an environment like that there is no real safety, only survival.

When I arrived at Cumberland, Maryland, the dominant group was from the District of Columbia, Maryland, and Virginia—DMV, the local name for the Washington metropolitan area. Men from Baltimore and Washington, D.C., controlled most of the power, so alliances were crucial. It didn't matter who you were before prison; what mattered was who you aligned with. Whether it was based on geography, religion, or gang affiliation, you needed to know where you stood.

At Elkton, the dynamics were different. A majority of the compound was run by men from Ohio. We held the geographic control, which shaped how things operated there. But no matter what prison you go to, men from Washington, D.C., always had a strong presence. Since no state prisons were in D.C., federal facilities became the only option, meaning a significant number of men from D.C. were within any compound. These regional dynamics created a unique balance of power that everyone had to navigate.

What most people can't see is that some men lose more than just their freedom in prison. They lose their sense of self, the self-respect they once had, and in some cases, they lose their lives. The scars left behind are not always visible but run deep. Some men turn to drugs to numb the pain, while others let it consume them.

Although policies may exist on paper, in reality, survival becomes a personal responsibility. Whether it's on the basketball court, in the dorms, or on the yard, inmates must navigate the world of prison with caution. Respect, alliances, and mental resilience are their tools for survival. Not everyone makes it out with their mind intact.

Important Facts:

- In 2024, 22 people in federal prisons died by suicide, highlighting the ongoing mental health crisis in correctional facilities (U.S. Department of Justice).

  www.justice.gov

- Suicide deaths in state prisons across the U.S. more than doubled in several systems between 2023 and 2024, marking one of the sharpest increases in recent years (Correctional Association of New York).

  www.correctionalassociation.org

- The suicide rate in U.S. prisons rose from 0.24 per 1,000 incarcerated individuals in 2013 to 0.76 per 1,000 in 2024, more than tripling over the past decade (Correctional Association of New York).

  www.correctionalassociation.org

HE WITHOUT SIN

Emotionally drained

Damn near insane

Who do I run to in a world full of pain?

It's always a battle to fight

When I get over one… another's in sight

COVID-19, police brutality

No job promotion, this is my reality

Brain overload, constantly fighting the system

No justice, no peace, I feel like a victim

Victimized by decisions

Victimized by the criminal justice system

Victimized by hate

Victimized by laws designed to segregate

"Stay strong, things will get better," that's what I hear
Well, you tell me why is being different something I fear?

Too much bitterness
Too much pain
I became a victim in the finger-pointing game

Built-up anger, built-up rage
It's a rocky road, one I didn't pave…
The one the government made
He without sin
Cast your own grave

CHAPTER 10

A System on Trial:
Breaking the Cycle

The American criminal justice system presents itself as a symbol of fairness and equality, but for who? For Blacks and other people of color lacking resources, it is usually a machine of coercion and submission, robbing inmates and their families of their rights and futures. Nearly 98% of federal cases never even make it to trial. Instead, defendants are forced into plea deals where fear outweighs any chance of a fair trial.

Prosecutors hold all bargaining power, offering deals that seem like the only way out. This is known as the "trial penalty," a system designed to punish anyone who dares to exercise their right to a trial, forcing them to accept plea deals to avoid harsher sentences.

I took a 20-year plea deal, not because I was guilty, but because the alternative was life in prison, a sentence that, in federal terms, means you will die behind bars. In my sentencing transcript, my date was not a release date; it was marked "deceased." The system forced me to make an impossible decision, I had no choice but to submit.

In federal drug cases, the "851 Enhancement" is a powerful tool prosecutors use to impose harsher mandatory minimum sentences based on prior convictions. For example, if you are caught with 50 grams or more of crack cocaine, the mandatory minimum sentence starts at 10 years. However, with one prior conviction, prosecutors can enhance that sentence to 20 years. With two prior convictions, they can enhance it to life in prison. In my case, because I accepted a plea deal, the prosecutors did not plan to file a second enhancement. But I didn't know until much later that even the initial 851 Enhancement had never been filed.

For an 851 Enhancement to apply, the prosecution must file it properly in court before trial or a guilty plea. The defendant and their lawyer must receive notice of the filing, allowing them to review and challenge it if necessary. The judge will then confirm that the notice was properly served and provide both sides an opportunity to address it before sentencing.

The day I accepted the guilty plea was the same day the prosecutor improperly applied the 851 Enhancement to my sentence. Without the proper filing or notice required for an 851 Enhancement, the prosecutor asked the judge to proceed directly to sentencing, and I was given 20 years.

In prison, I discovered this oversight. A jailhouse lawyer advised me to request my sentencing minutes. When I reviewed them, he pointed out that the 851 Enhancement was never filed. That discovery sparked my fight for freedom.

I began filing appeals, from 2255 motions to 2241 habeas petitions, tirelessly challenging the court's failure to file the 851 Enhancement. After nine years of relentless efforts, the Court of Appeals informed me that I had exhausted all legal remedies and could no longer file anything further in court.

When President Obama's crack law reforms passed in 2008, I thought I had a chance to reduce my sentence. However, because of the 851 Enhancement in my case, I was excluded. While others saw freedom in sight, I remained trapped by legal barriers, with my appeals exhausted. The crack law reforms reduced sentences for those without enhancements or complications, but for people like me, the fight was not over.

Refusing to be wrongfully defeated, I decided to take a different approach. I wrote directly to the judge, requesting a court-appointed attorney. Every prisoner has the right to legal representation, and the judge appointed Donna Grill, a public defender. Donna did something none of the private lawyers I paid over $100,000 ever did; she came to visit me. While those paid lawyers never met with me face-to-face to discuss my case, Donna sat down with me, listened to my story, and truly believed in my fight for justice.

For nine years, I battled the system, filing appeal after appeal, feeling like every legal avenue led to a dead end. But Donna's dedication changed everything. She dug into the details of my case, tirelessly advocating on my behalf. Her efforts finally got me back into court, and the result was a six-year reduction in my sentence.

After 14 years, I finally walked out of federal prison. But even then, the fight wasn't over. For those of us who manage to walk out of prison, the challenges are still there, but different. Reentry programs, though well-intentioned, often fail to address the harsh realities ex-felons face when trying to rebuild their lives.

Housing is one of the most immediate and pressing issues. Many landlords refuse to rent to individuals with a criminal record, leaving us to navigate housing markets with limited options. Even public housing programs, which are meant to provide stability, often exclude ex-felons entirely. This forces many to rely on family or friends, if they are blessed enough to have those connections. Otherwise, they are likely to end up homeless.

Securing employment with a felony conviction is an uphill battle. Many employers dismiss qualified applicants the moment they see "felony conviction" on a background check, trapping individuals in low-wage, unstable jobs or leaving them unemployed altogether.

The "War on Drugs" filled prisons with people like me, devastating communities of color. Mandatory minimums like the 100-to-1 crack versus powder cocaine sentencing disparity left judges with no discretion, disproportionately punishing Black Americans. Just 5 grams of crack cocaine carried the same sentence as 500 grams of powder cocaine, a disparity rooted in systemic bias. Even now, Black Americans make up 38.3% of the federal prison population, despite representing only about 14% of the U.S. population.

Locking up non-violent offenders for decades has not reduced crime. This systemic bias perpetuates cycles of poverty and dependence, making reintegration into society exceedingly difficult.

Think about this: 34 felony counts for falsifying business records tied to secret payments, and yet the outcome is no jail time, no fines, no consequences.

Now compare that to me and others like me, with fewer felony convictions, as we try to rebuild our lives. Doors are slammed shut, locking us out of opportunities before we even get the chance to redeem ourselves.

Meanwhile, someone with multiple convictions can rise to the most powerful position in the country. Make it make sense. This is unfair and unjust; it blatantly reveals how the system was built to keep the playing field uneven. Real change is not just overdue, but a responsibility we can no longer ignore.

It is time to dismantle the biases that stigmatize people with records and create opportunities, to ensure a system where second chances are not just slogans, but a reality for everyone willing to make the transition.

These challenges are not just systemic, they are deeply personal. Many of us return to communities where the stigma of incarceration follows us everywhere. It's not just about proving we have changed; it's about navigating a system designed to remind us of our past at every turn. Even something as simple as getting a driver's license or accessing education can feel like an insurmountable hurdle.

The same racial biases that fueled disproportionate sentencing don't disappear when it's time to reintegrate into society. They persist in the form of discriminatory hiring practices, limited housing opportunities, and systemic barriers that make starting over feel impossible. Programs that fail to tackle these barriers head-on are just extensions of the broken system, offering surface-level solutions to deeply rooted problems.

Reentry is more than just opening prison doors. It's about creating real opportunities for people to rebuild their lives with dignity, stability, and hope. Until we address these issues, we will continue to see families destroyed and communities struggling under the weight of a system that refuses to truly rehabilitate.

Even after I was released from federal prison, the fight wasn't over. I was sent to a halfway house, another form of incarceration that felt like an extension of the sentence I already served.

I went down to the prosecutor's office every day , determined to push for my full release. It wasn't just once or twice. I showed up for weeks. Finally, one day, the prosecutor stopped and asked, "I've seen you down here every day, how can I help?" That question felt like a door opening.

I explained my situation, laid out the details of my case, and showed him how much I knew about the legal complexities I was facing. He listened and said, "I can't make any promises, but I'll see what I can do." By the time I got back to the halfway house, the staff informed me that I was granted an immediate release. Finally, someone heard me.

Even then, I wasn't fully free. Ten years of probation loomed over me like a shadow. Once again, I didn't give up. I filed appeals, met with probation officers, and kept pushing for my freedom. For five long years, I fought. And eventually, it paid off. My probation was cut short, and for the first time in over 20 years, I tasted real freedom.

My story is not an isolated case, but the reflection of a system that wasn't built to rehabilitate, instead sustaining itself at the expense of human lives. For those of us who have been through it, the fight for freedom continues after walking out of prison. It lingers in every corner of our lives, where the scars of injustice remain long after the doors have opened.

Important Facts:

- 98% of federal criminal cases end in plea deals, leaving defendants with minimal opportunity to fully present their cases in court (Georgia Public Broadcasting).
  www.gpb.org

- The 100-to-1 sentencing disparity between crack and powder cocaine has historically targeted Black Americans disproportionately, though it was reduced to 18-to-1 by the Fair Sentencing Act of 2010 (Sentencing Project).
  www.sentencingproject.org

- Black Americans are incarcerated at nearly six times the rate of white Americans, highlighting racial disparities in the criminal justice system (National Conference of State Legislatures).
  www.ncsl.org

- Mandatory minimum sentencing laws contribute to overcrowded prisons and have disproportionately affected minority communities (Prison Policy Initiative). www.prisonpolicy.org

TRANSPARENCY

I took my life, bottled it up, and put it into poetry
Stitched my past up, rolled it into blunts to smoke for free
No longer worried 'bout who's for me
It takes skills to be real... living in poverty

Had to learn to hold my own
Didn't see many changes, working hard at 13 years old
Pops never told me the do's and don'ts
Not having... gave me a greater need to want

Wanted what was in the jeans
Wanted the money
Wanted the cream
Didn't want a sister or a brother as a crack fiend

It seems I wanted the American Dream...

But the prettiest people do the ugliest things

Classified as the ugliest of my team

A college grad, I choked my life out for the American cream

My life wasn't solid

Yet it stood on solid foundation

A taste of the streets

More money, more women the more I beat my feet

Gone 'til November...

Man, y'all dudes are clueless

I never wanted to leave

Selling drugs was foolish

I lost more than I ever could retrieve.

I couldn't afford old friends

All this damn stressin', I'm low on dividends

Even worse a friend turned me in

A dose of reality...

Back to where it all began

My life
The product of devious grins
Fake smiles on fake friends every weekend

Winning ain't everything...
It's the only thing
If I ain't winning
I'm losing chasing a pipe dream

My life
Now put your feet in my Nikes
A size 12...
It's bigger than you like
The price is life

CHAPTER 11

My Journey and the Call for Real Change

Education is often promoted as the key to breaking the cycle of recidivism, a lifeline to rehabilitation. On the surface, it seems like the perfect solution. But the reality tells a very different story. You cannot discuss reentry without addressing racism. Many of the individuals overseeing reentry programs are predominantly white, and the systemic biases that exist in society are mirrored within these systems through them.

The "education" is often superficial, designed to meet quotas rather than truly change lives. This failure was familiar to me. I experienced it long before prison, at Glenville High School in Cleveland, Ohio.

In my history class, the teacher, who also worked at Cuyahoga Community College better known as Tri-C, was rarely present. When he did show up, he handed out crossword puzzles instead of teaching. Trust me, we did not complain. We thought we were getting away with something by getting credit without doing the work. But in truth, we were being cheated out of an education. I had to teach myself what real history was beyond the surface-level mentions of Martin Luther King Jr. and Malcolm X. We did not realize at the time how much of our history was being withheld. The system failed us, and most of us didn't even realize it.

This same failure echoes in the so-called educational programs offered in prisons today. These programs are set up to create the appearance of progress, but there is a lack of depth and relevance needed to truly rehabilitate, especially for the diverse populations in prison.

In 2022, Black inmates accounted for 38% of the federal prison population, while Hispanic inmates made up 30%. Yet, educational programs fail to address the unique challenges and realities these communities face. They are not designed to help inmates re-enter society as healthy and productive citizens. Instead, they are created to "check the box" and satisfy institutional metrics.

The leadership and educational facilitators in these institutions don't often reflect the backgrounds of the people they are meant to serve. This disconnect makes it even harder for incarcerated individuals to receive support that could truly make a difference in their lives.

Institutions are often built in economically struggling rural communities, offering a lifeline of jobs and opportunities for local, mostly white residents. People who once worked in fast food restaurants or grocery stores can now apply to become correctional officers, gaining access to better pay and benefits. However, many of these individuals lack the training or cultural understanding needed to effectively interact with a diverse incarcerated population, creating an even greater divide within the system. Although rural areas benefit financially from these prisons, the inmates, disproportionately people of color, are left without resources they need to succeed.

Beyond jobs, the presence of a prison fuels economic growth in these rural areas. Stores, gas stations, and other businesses spring up to serve the influx of visitors, staff, and support services. Families traveling to visit their loved ones contribute to this local economy, spending money on fuel, snacks, and other necessities during their trips. These communities thrive on the revenue generated by incarceration, while inmates and their families bear the cost.

The sharp contrast between the economic gains of rural communities, and the lack of meaningful resources for those incarcerated, reveals the deeper inequities of the system. Prisons, for these towns, are an economic solution, but for the incarcerated, they represent a cycle of neglect and missed opportunities for true rehabilitation.

Here's the truth. Prison education should not just be about checking off requirements or handing out certificates. It ought to be about genuine transformation of the mind, heart, and spirit. Until the system acknowledges this, the promise of education in prison will remain unfulfilled, and the cycle of recidivism will continue.

Even after release, the barriers don't disappear. Society has ways of keeping people out, even when they have done everything possible to move forward.

For many, finding stable housing is one of the toughest challenges after incarceration. Even if you meet someone—a girlfriend or significant other who already has a place—that does not guarantee stability. If a landlord discovers your background and wants to be devious, he or she can refuse to allow you to stay there or even force their tenant to move out. I have seen people in these situations, struggling to hold onto any sense of normalcy.

Fortunately, my girlfriend (now wife) was doing well for herself when I moved in with her, and together we were able to create a loving home. Still, I know how different my story could have been.

For so many others, the housing reality is harsh, with landlords often denying applications outright when they see a criminal record, no matter how much progress has been made. It is a cycle that keeps people trapped, making it almost impossible to rebuild their lives.

The barriers I faced in the workforce were not because of my performance; they were built on my past. Despite my hard work and contributions, promotions were continuously denied. Deeply ingrained biases coupled with racism, discrimination block well-deserved opportunities, no matter how much you have paid your debt to society.

After years of working jobs that were not my passion, but necessary to support my family, I thought I found a role that aligned with my journey. I was hired to work in reentry as a Community Resource and Reentry Coordinator. In fact, I was only the second Black person ever hired by that company in nearly 25 years of its operation! It was a field I knew intimately, having walked that path myself.

My job was to simply connect inmates with resources that would support their reentry. This was supposed to be different. But in less than 90 days, I was forced out due to false accusations. I was accused of promoting false information and "selling insurance"—claims that were not only baseless but misleading. Medicaid and Medicare enrollment assistance is not the same as selling insurance. The accusation came from a man in a halfway house who was no longer in the program. Yet, his word was enough to have me immediately escorted off the compound and fired days later.

I was never given a chance to defend myself, explain what happened, or challenge the allegations.

I know firsthand how these programs often recycle the same faces, predominantly white, while true reform and representation are ignored.

White leadership often looks out for their own, whether those individuals are convicted felons or productive citizens. Meanwhile, Black individuals, especially those who bring authentic change and challenge the system, are often pushed aside. My presence brought real hope and connection to the men because they knew I understood their journey. However, that didn't matter. Clearly, these systems prioritize preserving their comfort zones over supporting genuine transformation.

Reentry mirrors the same systemic racism found in every other aspect of society. This was not an isolated setback, it was a blunt reminder of the deep-seated challenges people like me face every day, regardless of how much progress we make.

Unfortunately, my story is not unique, it is just one example of how reentry is not always about helping people rebuild their lives. There are countless others facing these same barriers, despite their potential, progress, and achievements.

Federal and state prisons, probation, parole, and reentry programs are in crisis. The entire structure built around incarcerating, monitoring, and supposedly helping people rebuild their lives is erroneous. From overcrowded prisons to underfunded and poorly managed reentry initiatives, the entire network often falls short of its purpose, leaving many without essential support that *could* help them truly transform their lives.

This crisis is not confined to one part of the system; it is woven into every layer, from sentencing to supervision, and incarceration to release. While we must address the broader structural failures, it is also important to recognize and support the programs and people effectively working and assisting others to succeed.

Although they may be few and far between, there are reentry organizations out there genuinely making a difference. These programs are focused on real rehabilitation, helping individuals regain their footing and reintegrate into society with dignity. I will highlight some of these resources in the back of this book, as they serve as examples of what true reentry work looks like.

Reentry often reflects the same racial inequalities Black people endure daily, even without a criminal record. However, for those who have been incarcerated, the stigma is amplified. When resources are limited, those in charge are more likely to prioritize helping white individuals navigate reentry over their Black counterparts. This uncomfortable truth about racial disparities in reentry must be acknowledged, exposed and addressed if we are to create real change.

Important Facts:

- U.S. Department of Justice, State Prison Education Statistics
  www.justice.gov

- RAND Corporation: The Effectiveness of Education in Reducing Recidivism
  www.rand.org

- Federal Bureau of Prison, Minority Incarceration Data
  www.bop.gov

- MCS-T.O.U.C.H.,
  Teaching Opportunity Unity by Connecting Hearts
  www.mcs-touch.org

DON'T EXPECT

Floating on a cloud of infinite possibility
Better judgment says beware, don't become a liability
Pushing against what is
As a man thinks so it is

Swimming against the current nothing is for sure
Life is unwanted pleasure, we openly endure

The soul attracts what it secretly harbors
Let go and let GOD's aspirations be your tomorrow

Trying to survive, swimming with a sense of pride
You get what you give, freedom denied

Aches and pains, digging the past from your mind
Burning your dreams like trash left behind

Mental health battles, isolation runs deep

Don't expect to become what you don't work to keep

Life is a journey, a chase for what's true

Destiny waits, but the work starts with you

CHAPTER 12

Emerging from the Shadows with a Purpose

I once stood in a courtroom and accepted a plea deal that meant 20 years of my life handed over to the federal system. I remember that agonizing moment. The air in the room so still you could almost hear my future being sealed. I stood there thinking, "This is the end of everything I know." But what I didn't understand then was that it was not the end, but the beginning of something far greater.

That day in the courtroom was the start of a journey that would push me beyond what I thought I could handle, by testing my faith, even bringing me to tears, but never breaking me.

The past could have weighed me down, chained me to regret, but I chose differently. I chose to rise, not just for myself, but for everyone who believed in me, for those who needed to see that change is possible, but most of all for my son and daughter. When the world tries to bury you, stand up! Every challenge, every setback, every year I thought was lost, became the fuel for something bigger.

Those years in the shadows could have stripped me down to nothing and left me hollow. But instead they shaped me. Those long and trying annual cycles did not just build me, they molded me with definition and strength like steel forged in fire. Every moment in the darkness sharpened me and gave me clarity. The shadows did not define me, but gave me the drive to step into the light—stronger, with a deeper sense of purpose than I ever imagined.

Stepping into freedom meant facing a world that moved on without me, but I wasn't interested in catching up to anyone else's expectations. I remember standing on the edge of freedom, just before walking through those doors, when someone said, "Don't try to catch up, just catch on." I held onto those words like a lifeline. My freedom wasn't about reclaiming what I had lost, but stepping into something new. And when I finally walked outside, it was as if the whole world opened up in front of me.

The air wasn't just air. It was fresh, yet thick with possibility. It filled my lungs in a way it never had before, as if every breath declared that I was alive. Everyone else was bundled up, shivering from the cold, but me? I was warm. That chill couldn't touch me. It was like I had been wrapped in the moment itself, standing there with my family, feeling free in a way that had nothing to do with walls or gates. That moment meant everything to me. I was breathing in my future.

Coming back into society after 14 years didn't mean "catching up," it was about "catching on." The world shifted. Sending an email and figuring out a smartphone were not hurdles, but new tools I had to master. And I did it the same way I had survived everything else, with persistence and determination.

Freedom wasn't just about walking outside. It was about claiming the space I stood in. Walking through my front door and opening my refrigerator were not just simple acts that most take for granted. They were milestones, each one a testament to everything I fought so hard for. Those moments were not only about being free, but living free.

Then came the joy, the kind of joy you can only feel after walking through that last prison gate. The first Thanksgiving was more than just a holiday, it was a homecoming. The first Thanksgiving in 14 years that my mom and I did not have to sit amongst strangers in the visiting room. Sitting at the head of the table, I was a part of the family, looking at the faces that stuck with me through every hard day. I felt as though I was truly seeing them for the first time. The laughter, the warmth, the clinking of glasses sounded like a symphony, a celebration.

Every moment was mine to hold on to for future reminiscing. Oh, and I can't forget about the food! It wasn't just a meal. It was the delicious taste of victory. The smiles, conversations, and love that flowed around the room. I could feel it all, deeper than ever before. A beautiful emotion I'll carry with me forever.

The joy of attending events like graduations, birthdays, and proms is priceless. I can now celebrate with my relatives instead of hearing about it over the phone or imagining myself there through pictures. These special moments reminded me of everything I lost and the happiness I've found in reconnecting with family.

The moments with my own son Edward and daughter Payton is a euphoria all its own. I feel such pride being able to witness my son become a responsible man who stayed far away from the path I went down. He is a devoted and loving father to my grandson, it's like watching two younger versions of myself, the best parts of me as a young man and as a toddler, exploring all this world has to offer. Being there to see my daughter graduate from high school, college and get married feels like a dream. There is nothing better as a girl dad than holding your baby girl's hand as you walk her down the aisle guiding her into the next phase of her life. Earning their forgiveness and receiving their love has been the highlight of my freedom.

Shortly after coming home in 2012, I moved to Columbus, Ohio with Giena and we got married in 2014. I understood that transformation sometimes means changing people, places and things. When some friends and family looked forward to me going back to my old ways, she only had one request - make an honest living to help contribute to our household. There was no pressure to bring in fast money. I was so relieved to have someone love me not for what I had or for who I used to be but for the man I am on the inside.

I gained three daughters, not stepdaughters. They are my daughters because I chose to love and help raise them. Sydney is now in her second year of college, while the twins Seleste and Selene dominate high school track with speed and determination. It's not about replacing what I missed, but embracing the second chance I have been given. I feel so lucky to be present in all of their lives, individually and collectively.

Despite there being a two foot difference in our height, some would say I am a carbon copy of my mom, or even her favorite (don't tell her other 9 children). My mom taught me what it means to have the faith of a mustard seed. During the days that crept by so slowly it felt like weeks, I channeled her unflinching spirit. I could hear her telling me "just keep it all in prayer". If there is no one else that I can count on in this world, I know I can count on my momma and her unconditional love. There is a priceless freedom, knowing that I can hear her voice at any time as opposed to scheduled phone calls. I often pop in on her unexpectedly just to get a hug or reminisce about my childhood. I love seeing her beautiful smile when she laughs. Yes, I have made it back to where I am supposed to be.

However, beyond the joy, beyond the family, lies one's purpose. Walking back into prison, not as an inmate, but as someone offering hope, I found a mission I never expected. Writing letters to the parole board, giving advice, being a voice for those still inside, is where my life took on new meaning. I hold onto this with everything I have.

Now, let's be clear. As emphasized before, this journey isn't just about me.

For 10 years, I worked with MCS-Touch, going into four different institutions across Ohio to facilitate programs.

These were not just classes where people showed up. They were spaces where real conversations happened, and we didn't just meet the requirements, but poured into each other. The success of a program is not measured by how many hours our participants sat during the discussions. It is measured by how deeply it impacts their lives.

There is a difference between checking off a requirement and genuinely investing in someone's growth. And that's the difference we need to focus on. Programs that don't just lock people away but give them the tools, support, and encouragement to rebuild their lives. That's what I've been working toward, both inside and outside prison walls.

We don't need more punishment. Real reform includes programs that teach men and women how to navigate life outside of prison, how to believe in their worth, and how to rise above the mistakes they've made. It's not just freedom from prison. It means embracing freedom to live and thrive, despite where you've been.

That's the mission I'm on. Not just for me, but for everyone still inside, for the families still carrying that weight, and for the communities waiting for their people to come home stronger, not broken.

So, what do you do when life comes at you hard? How do you rise when the world says you're finished? For me, it's about belief. Even on the extra tough days, make an unwavering decision to hold on, never giving up. I believe and accept, deep down, that no matter what comes my way, I've got the strength to keep pushing forward. And so do you.

Again, freedom is not just walking out of prison. It is standing outside on a cold night, breathing air that feels like a second chance. It is looking up at the stars, knowing that nothing is blocking your view anymore. Freedom is about the choices we make every single day. Each breath, each step forward, is built on the foundation of every challenge I've overcome, and each lesson I've learned.

Here's what I want you to take away. No matter where you've been, no matter what you've been through, the power to rise is already inside of you. Every setback is just a setup for a stronger comeback. I've been knocked down more times than I can count, but each time, I came back stronger. And I believe that you can, too.

This is not just my story, it is our story. We have all faced challenging situations that could've taken us out, but we're still here. We're still climbing. And as I close this book, I want you to remember: the journey isn't over. Not for me, not for you, not for anyone willing to keep pushing. Keep climbing, keep believing, and never stop fighting for the life you deserve.

The future is bright, not just for me, but for every person willing to believe they are more than their past. This is only the beginning. The key to freedom is already in your hands. The question is will you use it?

"We need leaders not in love with money, but in love with justice. Not in love with publicity, but in love with humanity."

— Dr. Martin Luther King Jr.

I Have a Dream Similar to Dr. King

I HAVE A DREAM

No more broken wings

No more hoping for things

The measure of a man is more than just bling and material things

I HAVE A DREAM

Not just for me as a man

But for my children, your children, our children

To stand hand-in-hand with other men

Like President Barack Obama and Senator Edward Kennedy

For human rights and equality

For a fair justice system and equal opportunity

41 shots weren't needed to shoot at me

Throw me in a jail cell and sodomize me

Swastika and noose hanging "Hang that nigga by a tree"

Man... that white woman was looking at me

"LIFE," I'm copping a plea

Economically, I HAVE A DREAM

Periodically, I want to raise my voice and let freedom ring

Let it scream, until I'm respected as a human being

Respected for the content of my character, not the color of my skin

But as I said, I HAVE A DREAM… and I'm gon' win

I HAVE A DREAM

Not to turn the other cheek

But to fight back if you raise your hand at me

To fight for equal protection under the law for BIPOC communities

I HAVE A DREAM

That health care be provided for everyone

And shelter is given to the homeless and the bum

I HAVE A DREAM

That one day Jews, Muslims, Christians, Jehovah's Witnesses,

I have a dream that all religions

Won't be divided but come together under one system

Have the same common goals and one common mission

I HAVE A DREAM

To stop the bloodshed in Ukraine

To bring our troops home from war

To open up those prison doors

Put money into run-down schools and help feed the poor

I HAVE A DREAM

To lower taxes and have fewer regulations

To sit down with rival crews and have a peaceful conversation

I HAVE A DREAM

To let my shoulder lean

Without the hassle of you and your team

Looking mean because I'm clean

I HAVE A DREAM

That one day, set tripping and gang banging

Standing on the corner curb, slanging, comes to an end.

That one day, Black-on-Black crimes cease

That racial profiling and police brutality become obsolete

I HAVE A DREAM

That the President signs a bill to end poverty

Giving our children a safer brighter road to be

It takes a nation to build a community

I HAVE A DREAM

That we fight with our pen

Instead of fighting with guns

Respect the opinion of another person

And the words from their tongue

I HAVE A DREAM

That one day, Blacks, Asians, Latinos, Jamaicans, and Whites

Can be productive politicians and senators in the same fight

I HAVE A DREAM

Where one day, racism doesn't exist

Where sexism isn't placed at the bottom of the list,

And haters… blown away with a kiss

I WISH… I WISH MY DREAM COMES TRUE

So I can scream

Scream from the top of my lungs at the mountaintop

Like Martin Luther King did too:

"Free at last, free at last

You better thank God Almighty

I'm not living in the past"

EPILOGUE

Let me be clear, the greatest danger to any society is when the guilty face no consequences. When the lawless feel untouchable, crime multiplies, accountability disappears, and injustice becomes normalized. That is the world we are living in today.

When most men and women leave prison, after years of accumulating small things like clothes, a watch, snacks, or even a little bit of pride, there are really only two possessions that matter when we walk out. Our pictures and our letters. Those are the only pieces that hold the weight of our stories, proof of who we are or who we were.

Yet, once we return to the outside world, the pull of material things often takes over. Cars, jewelry, liquor, or drugs may feel like relief, but they only provide a false comfort. They quiet the pain for a moment, but they never move us forward. Too often, they keep people revolving in the same cycles of hustling, crime, and survival in neighborhoods where opportunity is scarce. Let's be honest—these cycles are not accidents. They are products of systems designed to maintain inequality and destruction.

A few people manage to break through—Black men and women, other minorities, and the less fortunate who fight their way out of poverty—but compared to the masses still weighed down by these struggles, they are only a drop in the ocean.

Despite the barriers, the contributions of Black Americans and other minorities to this country cannot be denied. Black culture has shaped music, sports, and art worldwide. Minority entrepreneurs build businesses that employ millions. Black

Americans alone represent over $1.7 trillion in buying power each year, while Latino buying power surpasses $3 trillion. Minorities have fought in every American war, stood on the front lines of social movements, and continue to drive progress in education, technology, and public service. These are not small contributions. They are the backbone of America's growth.

Still, the weight of inequality remains heavy. Black Americans make up about 13% of the U.S. population but nearly 40% of the prison population. While the spending power of minorities fuels the economy, wealth is stripped from our communities almost as quickly as it is earned. Studies show that a dollar circulates in Asian communities for nearly a month, in white communities for more than two weeks, but in Black communities for only about six hours before it leaves. That imbalance is not by accident—it is by design.

I know this because I have lived on both sides. I know what it is to be weighed down by that life, and I also know what it means to make it out. For me, making it out means I did not become another recidivism statistic. It means I now own my own company, I have written books, and I am known in my community for the work I do.

Even now, as I sit here writing this book, I am still carrying pain. Writing has been my therapy, but it has also been a mirror. It forces me to confront the wounds I continue to carry every single day.

This is my reality. While struggle is universal, it is not equal. Most white people cannot fully understand what it means to live under the constant weight of systemic oppression.

They can imagine it, compare it to their own struggles, but for some of us, the fight begins at birth. It is written into our skin color, our zip code, our social background.

So, why am I writing this book? I ask myself that often. History shows us that Black leaders who dare to speak out are silenced, discredited, or murdered. Yet, I cannot stay silent. Especially not in a world where insurrectionists— people who attacked the very heart of our democracy—walk free, pardoned, and celebrated.

Here is the truth I hold onto: change is still possible. The challenges faced by incarcerated individuals and those reentering society are immense, but they are not insurmountable. With active participation, real reform, and community support, we can disrupt these cycles. Each of us has a role to play, whether it is fighting for criminal justice reform, supporting reentry programs, or mentoring the next generation so they never enter the system in the first place. That is why I wrote this book. Not just to tell my story, but to invite you into the fight for something greater.

Below are key organizations and resources where you can get involved, stand against injustice, and help build a future where reentry means renewal, not relapse, where incarceration does not mean erasure, and where justice is not just a promise, but a practice.

As I close, I want to leave you with this. My story is only one story, but it carries a message that belongs to us all.

TRANSFORMATION IS POSSIBLE.

Justice is worth fighting for. The work is not finished until every Black man and woman, every brother and sister of every color, every child, every elder, and every person of faith or no faith can walk free, not just from prison, but into a life of dignity, opportunity, and hope. Real change will come when we learn to see each other as part of the same human family, playing our parts together like instruments in one band, creating a harmony that drowns out division, and builds a future louder than hate and stronger than fear.

Resources for Reentry and Criminal Justice Reform

Take action. Each of these organizations is dedicated to making a difference in reentry success, justice reform, or preventing incarceration by supporting at-risk youth. Explore their websites, volunteer, donate, or advocate. Your involvement can create real change in your community.

- Equal Justice Initiative (EJI)
  Providing legal representation to individuals who have been illegally convicted, unfairly sentenced, or abused in state prisons and jails, while also working to challenge racial and economic injustice.

<u>www.eji.org</u>

- National Reentry Resource Center

  A comprehensive hub offering evidence-based strategies, tools, and resources to support successful reentry, reduce recidivism, and improve outcomes for people returning to communities.

  <u>www.csgjusticecenter.org/nrrc</u>

- Prison Fellowship

  Restoring those affected by crime and incarceration through biblically based programs, advocacy, and support, transforming lives inside and outside of prison walls.

  <u>www.prisonfellowship.org</u>

- The Fortune Society

  Supporting successful reentry with holistic services including housing, employment, education, and counseling, helping individuals with justice involvement rebuild their lives.

www.fortunesociety.org

- REFORM Alliance (Probation, Parole & Systemic Justice Reform)

  Transforming probation and parole by changing laws, systems, and culture to create real pathways to work and wellbeing.

  https://reformalliance.com

- American Civil Liberties Union (ACLU)
  Defending civil rights and liberties through litigation, advocacy, and public education, fighting to ensure fairness, justice, and equality under the law.
  www.aclu.org

- LeBron James Family Foundation
  Empowering children and families through education, mentorship, and community programs, including the groundbreaking I PROMISE School in Akron, Ohio.
  www.lebronjamesfamilyfoundation.org

- The Boys and Girls Clubs of America
  Providing safe spaces, mentorship, and programs in academics, leadership, and healthy living to help young people reach their full potential.
  www.bgca.org

- The My Brother's Keeper Alliance
  An initiative of the Obama Foundation focused on creating pathways to success for boys and young men of color through mentorship, education, and community engagement.
  www.obama.org/mbka

- The Innocence Project
  Working to exonerate wrongfully convicted individuals through DNA testing and reforming the criminal justice system to prevent future injustices.

www.innocenceproject.org

- Year Up
  Bridging the gap between talent and opportunity by providing young adults with training, internships, and skills to launch meaningful careers.
  www.yearup.org

- Think Make Live Youth (Columbus, Ohio)
  Empowering youth through mentoring, life-skills training, and leadership development to inspire change and build brighter futures.
  www.thinkmakelive.org

- Van Jones Advocates Pass Nonpartisan Criminal Justice Reform
  Highlighting Van Jones' efforts to bring together leaders across political lines to push for meaningful

reforms that reduce incarceration and create fairer justice policies.

www.standtogether.org/stories/criminal-justice/van-jones-advocates-pass-nonpartisan-criminal-justice-reform

- The Frederick Douglass Project is Helping to Reduce the U.S. Recidivism Rate

  Fostering dialogue and connection between incarcerated individuals and the outside community to reduce stigma, build empathy, and lower recidivism.

  www.standtogether.org/stories/criminal-justice/the-frederick-douglass-project-is-helping-to-reduce-the-us-recidivism-rate

- Nonprofits Actively Reducing Recidivism

  Showcasing organizations nationwide that are making a measurable impact by addressing the root causes of recidivism and supporting successful reentry.

  www.standtogether.org/stories/criminal-justice/nonprofits-actively-reducing-recidivism

- Reentry Support Project (RS Project)

Providing direct reentry services, mentorship, and resources to individuals returning home from incarceration, reducing barriers and promoting long-term success.

www.rsproject.us

- Real Men Real Talk Podcast (African American Male Wellness Agency)

    A safe space for honest conversations about mental health and wellness in Black men, breaking the stigma and encouraging growth, healing, and self-care.

    https://aawellness.org/real-men-real-talk-podcast/

- MAGNET (Manufacturing Advocacy & Growth Network)

    Helping small and mid-size manufacturers grow through expert consulting services and a strong network of industry partners, creating opportunities for innovation and success.

    https://www.manufacturingsuccess.org/

About the Author

Edward A. Julian, Sr is an author, poet, and advocate who has turned 14 years of incarceration into 14 years of impact, teaching, and transformation. Since his release, he has dedicated his life to empowering others through writing, speaking, and reentry education. He is the author of *Begin, Believe, Become: The 3-Step Process to Transformation and Achievement.*

The Begin Within Initiative Life Skills Course has guided countless individuals—both youth and adults—toward growth, accountability, and success. Edward's work extends beyond books and classrooms. He has served as a credible messenger, a group facilitator, and a mentor, impacting students, returning citizens, and communities across Ohio. His unique perspective as someone who has lived on both sides of incarceration gives him credibility and insight few can match. Today, he continues to lead through his company, The Begin Within Initiative, LLC, and the nonprofit Begin Believe Become Foundation for change. Above all, he is a husband, father, and grandfather, driven by faith and a commitment to ensure others know that their past does not define their future.

YOU

I remember the day that **you** were born and God put **you** on this earth.
I held you close and said a prayer and thanked him for your birth.

It's **you** who has given me a reason to live and added value to my life.
And when times got rough, like locked in this cell, because of **you** I continued to fight.

As I recall my thoughts when I'm thinking of **you**, like the first time **you** called me daddy.
Or remember the time **you** took your first steps, such precious times we've had.

It's **you** that I promised, my oath for life, to never leave your side.
But the oath has been broken, cause I'm locked in prison and **you** feel my oath was a lie.

I know that it's **you** who suffers the most and paying the cost for my greed.
I was hungry for wealth, the cash and fast life, and trying to provide for your needs.

But I was still young, with a lot of responsibilities, running without a plan.
So if I have hurt **you**, or caused **you** pain and upset **you**, please forgive me, I'm only a man.

You must keep your faith, and pray every night, cause one day this nightmare will end.
And when it does, I'm coming straight home, and the gaps we can start to mend.

So until that day comes I'm sending **you** my love and this is from the heart.
There is nothing that exists, fence nor miles, that can keep two souls apart.

And when you're lying in bed thinking of your dad, and wondering is he thinking of **you** too.
Don't trouble your mind, because your one of a kind, and my heart and mind are with YOU!

love Daddy

P.S. I Miss You

Sad Times & Good Times
Love Daddy

*Above is a letter I wrote to my daughter during my incarceration, one of the many
ways I tried to stay connected to her despite the distance.*

Edward A. Julian, Sr.

www.ingramcontent.com/pod-product-compliance
Lightning Source LLC
Chambersburg PA
CBHW021235130626
46554CB00004B/1509